A Woman of Her Time

A Woman of Her Time

Memories of My Mother

LOUISE DUPRÉ

translated by **LIEDEWY HAWKE**

Original version published in French as *L'album multicolore*, 2016.
Copyright © 2016 by Les éditions Héliotrope, Montreal.
Copyright © Liedewy Hawke 2020 for the English translation.

All rights reserved. No part of this book may be reproduced, for any reason or by any means, without permission in writing from the publisher.

Copyediting: Kaiya Cade Smith Blackburn
Author photo: Mélissa Giguère
Cover image: Courtesy Louise Dupré
Cover design: Debbie Geltner
Book design: Tika eBooks

Library and Archives Canada Cataloguing in Publication

Title: A woman of her time : memories of my mother / by Louise Dupré ; translated by Liedewy Hawke.
Other titles: Album multicolore. English
Names: Dupré, Louise, 1949- author. | Hawke, Liedewy, translator.
Description: Translation of: L'album multicolore.
Identifiers: Canadiana (print) 20190224975 | Canadiana (ebook) 20190224983 | ISBN 9781773900483 (softcover) | ISBN 9781773900490 (HTML) | ISBN 9781773900506 (Kindle) | ISBN 9781773900513 (PDF)
Subjects: LCSH: Dupré, Louise, 1949-—Family. | LCSH: Paré, Cécile, 1914-2011. | CSH: Authors, Canadian (French)—Québec (Province)—Biography | LCSH: Mothers and daughters—Québec (Province) | LCSH: Québec (Province)—Biography. | LCGFT: Autobiographies.
Classification: LCC PS8557.U66 Z46 2019 | DDC C841'.54—dc23
Printed and bound in Canada
Legal deposit – Library and Archives Canada and Bibliothèque et Archives nationales du Québec, 2020

The publisher gratefully acknowledges the support of the Government of Canada through the Canada Council for the Arts, the Canada Book Fund, and of the Government of Quebec through Société du développement culturel (SODEC).

We acknowledge the financial support of the Government of Canada through the National Translation Program for Book Publishing, an initiative of the Action Plan for Official Languages – 2018-2023: Investing in Our Future, for our translation activities.

Linda Leith Publishing
Montreal
www.lindaleith.com

To my family,
In memory of Cécile

Table of Contents

I. The Fragrance of Chrysanthemums — 1

II. Snapshots — 51

III. The Grace of the Day — 129

References — 177

I

The Fragrance
of Chrysanthemums

I look at my mother in her bed. She is white, as white as the sheet. She has just died, and I don't believe it. The nurse beside me doesn't either. Only an hour ago he told me about a protocol to be followed soon, during the stage of respiratory distress. "Distress," the word hit me like a punch. She may have heard while she slept, she may have decided to leave us before. I am relieved. That is how I feel while I look at my mother, her face peaceful now, still warm, as though she were lost in a happy dream.

In the evening, pain pounced on her like an animal. It began to devour her insides. I asked the nurse to call the doctor. He agreed to increase the dose of morphine—one doesn't let a ninety-seven-year-old woman die in agony. She finally dozed off. Standing at her bedside, I wept over her, I wept over the billions of living beings, humans of all races, animals of all species, who have died, since the beginning of time, after much suffering. Who is this God who is supposed to be infinitely good and kind?

I stroke my mother's face. You should talk to someone who has just died, I have heard. Consciousness isn't like the heart, which stops all at once. It slowly fades. I don't know if there is any foundation to this belief, but I talk to my mother, I tell her I love her. It's easier for me than when she was alive, she never liked great emotional outpourings. Except these past weeks. She couldn't control her feelings as well, she smiled when I hugged her, she let herself be tucked in at night, at bedtime.

I am waiting for my two brothers. They shouldn't be long. I woke them up a few minutes ago. I didn't need to explain. The ringing of the telephone was enough. The nurse asks me if he should rearrange my mother in the bed. No, no staging. She should remain just as she is. My brothers should see her as I saw her. He leaves, and the room is silent again. I can finally think about my mother, think about her death. For a long time, I imagined a theatrical scenario: she looks at me, I hold her hand, and she is fully conscious when she takes her last breath. I would never have thought death could be so ordinary. You get a morphine injection and you fall asleep, as after a hard day.

Afterwards, who are you? A soul, a ghost, a dispossessed body, a shadow, a portrait gradually blurring, a memory, a name on a gravestone? I cannot take my eyes off my mother's now unwrinkled face. The marks of living have been erased. Under cover of icy darkness, I let myself slip with her into a time that is perfectly smooth. Forever still.

I keep vigil over my dead mother. Am I alone keeping vigil here? A few minutes ago, for the morphine, I walked up the dark corridor to the nursing station, and through a half-open door I caught a glimpse of a young woman. She was writing in her bed. So, you could write here, in the oppressive silence of this postoperative department. I brought that image with me, as if it could give me courage.

I don't need courage anymore. No longer seeing my mother suffer the way she suffered this evening is the only reality that allows me to accept her death. It is my consolation. In the late afternoon, the doctor predicted the onset of peritonitis. That's what must have happened. But we won't be sure, there will be no autopsy. Her body will decompose in peace at the cemetery, near that of my father. Our whole childhood under one gravestone.

I think of us, my mother's children, as a unit. "The children," she used to say even when we were grown-up, grouping us in a single picture. She loved us with the love of a woman who had passionately wanted children. And we loved our mother deeply. This is what matters in the pale light of our last moments alone with her. The flashes of irritation, of impatience, of anger, and the misunderstandings I may have had with her over the years, have vanished like the wrinkles in her face. A perfect mother slowly grows cold in the white bed.

I wish my brothers would not come. I wish no one would come to get my mother. I would like to remain alone with her, for all eternity. I don't cry anymore, I am dazed. She isn't gone, my mother is there, very much present in death, the death I asked for all evening. Her absence will slyly creep up on me when her body will be taken away. That's what I expect. I have been preparing myself for it since November, to spare myself the worst. Illness, for example. So many women fall ill after their mother's death. Will my body be able to cope with the grief?

A sudden creaking noise, the door is pushed open. My brothers. The room is alive again. We are together once more, as we were fifty years ago, my mother in our midst. Perhaps she can hear us, perhaps our voices reach her from a great distance, through a fog. We will keep vigil over her until they come and take her away from us. Bodies must be left in the room for two hours after death has been pronounced. That is the law. In case they weren't really dead? In case they came back to life? The doctor hasn't been yet. I'm glad. We will have our mother to ourselves till dawn.

Not a sound on the floor. The patients all appear to be asleep. We talk about her in hushed voices, we reminisce. Then we start discussing the funeral. A church service or a secular ceremony? Did she want to be buried? Cremated? We don't know her last wishes. During the long days I spent with her these past weeks, I tried to find out. I didn't succeed. I must have been too vague. But can you ask direct questions of someone who is already no more than a shadow? Not me, not to *that* mother.

As if she had read my mind, she said while having her tea, "in less than three years, I'll be a hundred years old." I nodded, trying to believe it too. But my faith soon gave way to doubt. Since the summer, she had been deteriorating rapidly. How would she be in a few months? Would she live to be a hundred, like those living dead on the front page of newspapers?

My brothers seem relieved as well. There are times when wishing for death is an act of love. We tell stories from the long-ago days when she was our all-powerful mother. We take turns going up to the bed, we caress her, kiss her. We have become her brood again, her nestlings waiting for the daily feeding. Not for long. The doctor's arrival tears us away from our childhood. He asks us to leave. He wants to proceed with the pronouncement of death.

Our mother is well and truly dead. The doctor confirms what we already know. He gives her wedding-ring to one of my brothers, who holds it out to me. I slip it on my finger and clench my hand. It's as if another life has just entered my veins. I feel ready to face reality on my own. For the first time, I glimpse my own death in a hospital bed on an icy December night. But there is no fear rushing through me, no sadness. All I ask for is strength, the strength needed to cope with fractured time.

★★★

I got up this morning feeling as though I had lived beside my mother without knowing her, without an awareness of who she was before she became my mother. *Before*, as a child, a teenager, a student with the Sisters of the Congrégation Notre-Dame, her first loves, her job in an office, her years in Toronto, her going out with my father, the early days of her marriage. All the times in a life that exist side by side and complete one another can turn into a jumble, but when you fit them into a frame, they end up forming a more or less coherent portrait. I went to get my laptop, brought it to bed with me and began this narrative. "Writing is my prayer. Writing is my prayer to the dead," stated Madeleine Gagnon. A left-handed prayer that slowly opens a secret wound, buried in silence. Will writing, although I haven't known how to pray for a long time, give me a spirituality that some call faith?

I am very much my mother's daughter. She didn't believe in God. Her father didn't either. A memory of when I was five surfaces in my mind: the doctor has just left. My grandmother's eyes are red. "We'll have to send for the priest," she says. My mother nods, she doesn't know I'm listening, she doesn't have time to pay attention to me. I hear "haemorrhage," which must be a terrible word because right after that, she says, "he is going to die." I'm behaving myself, I play with my little brothers, I don't cry. My mother paces back and forth between the bathroom and the bedroom where my grandfather lies. He is vomiting up blood. We're not allowed to go and bother him. We stay in the living room. There is a knock on the door. A man in a long black robe walks in. It's a priest—I know because I go to Mass on Sunday. He enters the bedroom, then I see him come out again just a few minutes later. My grandfather has refused to receive the last rites. He has lived without God, he will die without God.

My mother spent the last four decades of her life without God. Yet shortly before she died, in certain lucid moments, she began to wonder. There were times when I answered that yes, perhaps our soul will survive us, perhaps it will. What do we know about it? But my cheeks would flush, as when I told her lies when I was a little girl. Childhood is never far behind us when we face our mother.

I used to think it was going to be easier to write about her after her death. I would no longer be afraid of upsetting her, I wouldn't have to protect her anymore. I would be able to tell the unvarnished truth. But what *is* the truth? I would like to stick to the facts as much as possible, capture my memory of her intact, bring her back to life, her every gesture, her every word, her strong beliefs and casual opinions. Actually, if I were honest with myself, I would have to admit that I am attempting the impossible. I am deluding myself. And yet I persist, I go deeper into my delusion.

I ask myself for whom I will write this narrative. For my daughter, grandson, my brothers, sisters-in-law, my nephews, my niece? But the woman I saw die will always only be *my* mother. I felt this intensely at times in the months when we took turns staying with her. And even long before. We occupied different spaces in her mind. She didn't mention the same things to all three, didn't confide in us equally. She kept silent with any one of us about some aspects of her health. We liked to think she suffered from memory loss. She mistrusted us, in fact. With good reason. As she showed more and more signs of senility, we worried about her, and she sensed it. Angry at us when we had to look after her affairs, she called me sometimes. "I can still do it," she would say. "What idea have you got into your head?" Isn't it awful to think that at the end of your life you come to look upon the children you have carried, raised, and loved, as your enemies?

In the final weeks, she didn't understand why we were anxious to stay with her. With neighbours rallying around, attendants, a cleaning lady, cooks, the manager, the caretaker, the telephone, and her emergency button, what could possibly happen to her? Why be afraid she might stumble with no one coming to her aid for several hours? "You could fall in your bathroom too," she would say. In the beginning, I reminded her of her cardiovascular incident and I insisted, her doctor was worried too. What if she broke a hip? But she'd forget, she wanted to forget. So, I stopped mentioning it. My mother had become like a child. My child?

There is a world of difference between a toddler we see growing up and a woman who is fading away. When I was with my mother, hour after hour, sadness overwhelmed me.

She awoke later and later each morning. I would slowly push her bedroom door open around nine. When she slept, she already had the facial expression of death. With a pounding heart, I listened for her breathing, then closed the door again, reassured and disappointed. To die in her sleep, in the bed that had followed her all her married life, the bed where she first made love, where she conceived us, that is what I wanted for her. And for us. Then she would never know the depressing life inside a nursing home. We would have to make a decision soon. We couldn't go on taking turns for months on end in that apartment in our old home town. But we kept delaying the moment of truth, hoping for a miracle. The miracle didn't happen.

I would rather have seen my mother dead than tell her, "You are leaving this place." She was born a few hundred metres away, in a duplex, now demolished. A little later her parents had a house built on a nearby street. That is where she was brought up, and so were we, her children, after our grandfather died. And like us, her oldest grandchildren slept, ate, and played there. After my father's death, my mother went back to live very near to where she was born. For twenty-eight years, she had lived in that building. It had recently been turned into a seniors' residence, with the usual services: a dining-room, cleaning lady, and nurse.

Sherbrooke was her whole life. She pronounced it the English way, as in the past, when the town still remembered its Loyalist origins. At the threshold of adulthood, the three of us left the town. Work took us elsewhere, but we often returned to Sherbrooke to visit her. *She* would only leave town for special occasions, such as a family celebration, or a funeral. Each time, it was a wrench for her. But the day drew near when we would have to force her to leave everything behind, to come and live near one of us. The day was approaching when we just wouldn't be able to go on. No doubt it would kill her. I dismissed that idea from my mind the way I used to drive away bad thoughts when I was twelve.

At what age can you take the risk of killing your mother? We weren't taught that in school. Parents used to die younger, that's true. No one lived to be a hundred. I belong to the first generation that faces this question and has to find an answer. Or waits until the answer is an obvious, inescapable fact.

Perhaps I am writing this narrative with the hidden purpose of being forgiven.

★★★

My mother's death left me without a voice, without sadness, without hope. As if I had been exiled to the Arctic wilderness. I am doomed to wander alone. I walk on in the whiteness, I go around in circles within the deadened places of my memory, unable to project myself into any future. I stay in my bedroom for hours, my eyes fixed on a drawing by Louise Robert. Fine black lines, pastel forms, scribbles, pinkish spots looking like faded drops of blood, and a grey, opaque window that doesn't allow the slightest glimpse of the landscape. At the bottom of the picture, in big red letters, this inscription: "It could have been in a dream." Yes, it is as if that night of December 30th, 2011 has been a dream, an invention, pure fiction. My mother isn't dead, you don't die without saying your farewells. You anticipate, you let people know, you leave your last wishes, you say what kind of funeral you would like. When you are a mother, you protect your children to the very end. But if you act that way, it is because you see death coming, you can recognize it.

My mother had a remarkable capacity for denial. She had given birth to her three children without labour pains. She hadn't suffered during menopause, no palpitations, no hot flashes, no discomfort. In November, she hadn't had a cardiovascular incident, she had no difficulty walking. She ordered me to go home. She accused me, I saw the dark side of everything, I brooded needlessly. Why not trust in life? I felt my blood boiling. I tried to control myself. I mustn't explode. Above all, not explode. I mustn't add pain to pain. Do you blow up at a woman who has been driven back against a grey, opaque window?

Yes, I am anxious, fearful, a worrier. I am not particularly proud of that. It has taken me years to come to grips with what I am. My mother knew exactly how to aggravate me. But I got my anxiety from *her*. "Be careful," she kept telling me, without saying a single word. She had a nerve, criticizing me for something I got from her. Or else, she was being utterly thoughtless. Or perhaps she felt so powerless that she was no longer able to show consideration for the people she loved. A good offense is the best defense, isn't it?

She wasn't wrong, we had become traitors. We couldn't leave everything behind to go and spend weeks at her apartment. Sometimes, in lucid moments, she realized that, and admitted in a defeated voice, "This can't go on." With a sinking feeling, I would agree. A few minutes later, she had forgotten. The very next day there would be the same words, the same arguments, a glimmer of hope that something we said might finally register in a recess of her memory, that she might consent to leave her apartment.

I would take her blood pressure, wash her, cook her meals, cut up her meat. I made her use her walker when she went to the bathroom. I took her to her bedroom for her afternoon nap. I tucked her in at bedtime, watched her at night when she got up to go to the toilet. I dialled her friends' phone numbers for her. My long-ago eldest-daughter reflexes surfaced again. To watch my little brothers, keep them entertained, comfort them. What my mother called *being reasonable*. To give in, to forgive. I quickly learnt to put reason before angry outbursts.

In the two months that my mother's deterioration lasted, I hoped for tears the way one hopes for rain during a drought. Nothing, though. Numbness. I talked and functioned, but I was going through the motions of daily life like a robot. I looked after my mother with a heart of stone. I lived through those two months haunted by an image—that of my mother walking out of her apartment for the last time, leaving behind the furniture she inherited from her parents. Her treadle sewing machine, her silver cutlery, her knickknacks, porcelain cups, the out-of-tune piano with the yellowed reproduction of Degas's ballerinas above it. All those objects that had witnessed our childhood, our love affairs, our first break-ups, our worries as new parents, our disappointments. Cut off from her small world, my mother would no longer be anything but a shattered old woman. We too would have to give up our past.

I hid the truth from her to the very end. On the morning she was to leave for Quebec City, where my younger brother lives, I called on all the parts I had played in college, where I did some acting. In a reassuring voice I told her I had to go home, to Montreal, to take care of my grandson. Fortunately, my brother and sister-in-law were inviting her to come and spend Christmas with them. On New Year's Day we would all be together. I didn't explain where that celebration would take place. I must have been convincing, she willingly went along with the plan, she chose to think she would soon be back in her own home. The lie had some merit, she wouldn't feel she was crossing her doorstep for the last time. But as she was about to leave, my mother, suddenly wanting to look stylish, asked me to straighten the mohair beret on her head, then she cast a lingering glance in the mirror above the chest of drawers in her bedroom, and whispered, "Today I am leaving my apartment." Did she mean, *For good*? *For a few days*? Perhaps she had been playing the game, too. She may in fact have been more lucid than I thought.

When I kissed her in the car, I didn't know I would find her a week later stuffed with morphine in a hospital room. I didn't know she wouldn't celebrate New Year's Day with us. I didn't want to see death coming either. I must have sensed what the poet Paul Bélanger put into words: "...when the mother dies, she takes humanity with her."

★★★

Writing is resisting me. It has never resisted me so much. Reticence? Difficulty accepting the facts? A refusal to accept that I have lost my mother? I drag every sentence out of some kind of fog where I hear an echo reverberating a thousand times of words I am unable to catch, as if they were spoken in an unknown language. In the morning I sit down at my keyboard and wait. I wait for a first gleam, a glimmer, a quavering series of sounds, a soothing rhythm lighting up my mother's cold, stiff face. Ensnared by death, I cannot write. I have to fight against the image of my mother being forever apart from me, from my brothers, our childhood, our birthplace. I must be unrelenting. I must challenge her absence. Every morning, I rekindle my memory. Every morning, I must dip into grief.

Since the night of December 30th, life has taken up all the space. The funeral, the thank-you notes, and the inevitable cleaning of the apartment, whose keys I had to return. I volunteered. Wasn't that the best way to face the bereavement? I sorted, threw things out, filled boxes and boxes with clothes, dishes, and several small objects I couldn't part with. They were ordinary, often useless things—an old wallet, a painting by a woman who lived next door, a chipped statuette of the Blessed Virgin. And suddenly some object would devastate me. Papa's thermos or the Gattuso olive jar in the shape of an owl that had served as a piggy bank. Had it belonged to one of my brothers or to me? Mama had difficulty making ends meet and did what she could to spoil us.

We had been slow in having a telephone and television at home, we counted every penny. My father had been ill for months and Mama needed to withdraw money from her insurance policy to pay back the hospital. She settled the debt at the rate of two or three dollars a month. No health cards in the fifties. Until her dying day Mama remembered the Duplessis era. She would be indignant about people who wanted to turn back the clock. Getting medical care, getting an education—to her this was a matter of justice, not a privilege.

All it had taken was that old piggy bank for a whole stretch of time to come back to life. The days of the family home, 1ère Avenue Nord, where we had gone to live with my grandmother after my grandfather died. A beautiful two-storey house, built in 1923. Oak floors, Douglas fir panelling, glass doors, a garden we could run in, squirrels, robins, and a tawny cat that, amazingly, had given birth behind the velvet sofa. Three kittens we were mad about.

Later, I would have liked to live in a brand new bungalow, as did some of my girlfriends. Our house was old, my grandmother's furniture out of fashion. My mother made everything herself, dresses, coats, the boys' jackets, scarves, mittens, curtains, tablecloths, and coverlets. She never went to the hairdresser's, always perming her hair herself. The spirit in our house was one of economy and resourcefulness. I haven't forgotten. Money problems in your childhood are something you never forget.

"We weren't rich, but we were happy," my mother murmured one evening, decades later, in the dimly lit living room. To reassure her, I quickly agreed. It was probably true because I had never asked myself the question. I didn't search for what was beneath that sentence. My mother grew up in a certain comfort. Her father had the house built on 1ère Avenue Nord, he bought a Ford, which he kept until the 1929 Depression. Then he was forced to choose between the house and the car. His tailoring was bringing in less money, but enough to support his family.

My mother had seen what money problems meant. Neighbours going daily to the soup kitchen, a friend who lost all his money, my grandmother making hats for poverty-stricken little girls. My mother would soon start working for a starvation wage herself. She grew used to watching every penny and had kept on doing so. If she broached the subject with me, it was because she worried about us. It must have been difficult to accept that her children weren't as well-off as she had been as a child.

We weren't destitute, our circumstances were like those of most working-class children. We ate at every meal, we had boots, warm coats. In the afternoon, my mother would take apart old garments given by the aunts and lay the pieces flat on the table to cut them while following the shape of the pattern she had bought. When we were finally in our beds at night, she would lift the cover of her sewing machine and make new clothes for us, which she trimmed with whatever she could find, velvet, corduroy, fur. A little coat with a cape edged with grey Persian lamb, for example. I must have been six.

And that red check dress for going to school. Even the teacher in first grade complimented me on that. It was a snowy morning. I apologized for having given only a penny for the Sainte-Enfance. I would bring a silver coin when my father would be well again. I still clearly remember my uneasiness, a kind of vague shame. "That's a lovely dress you are wearing," Mme G. said. I answered that my mother made it, filled with pride all of a sudden.

She wasn't just being polite, I could tell, my mother sewed very well. She helped her father when she was young. He had studied dressmaking in New York for two years.

My grandmother made hats. She was a milliner. She had imagination, a bold streak, a sense of humour, modern ideas. At the beginning of the twentieth century, a young girl from a good family wasn't supposed to work. It was frowned upon. But in spite of her mother's objections, Léda left Nicolet to make a life for herself, as she put it. She found work in a shop in Drummondville. There she met Bruno, fell madly in love with him. They married. They got along well, they did similar work. Today, they would be part of the fashion world. Their jobs would be glamorous. At the time, their trade didn't have the prestige it has now.

We talked about dressmaking every day in our house. I used to accompany my mother to choose patterns, remnants on sale, buttons, ribbon. She made blouses for me until her eighty-fifth year and sewed clothes for herself almost to the end. Everyone was involved in her projects, in her dreams of elegance and beauty. One bleak January evening, we had to pile dresses, skirts and suits into boxes so we could give them to a charity organization. All those hours of work! I tried to think of the destitute women who would be wearing them, they would surely be glad to have them. The thought was no consolation to me.

That familiar sound, the creaking of a sewing-machine treadle lulling us to sleep in the evening, between sheets that smelled of the clothes line—how many people will hear it as they read this, how many women in Quebec sewed late into the night in those days? How many garments given by aunts were taken apart and resewn every year? With that machine my mother taught me how to sew as soon as I was old enough not to drive the needle into my finger, just as she showed my daughter after me. The machine is now unusable. And the cover is cracked, I wouldn't even be able to donate it to a museum. But I couldn't bring myself to put it out with the garbage. It vibrates still, thanks to my mother's lack of sleep, thanks to that of all the women of her era who wanted the best for their children.

The old Singer has made its way to Montreal. It rests in peace at my place, under a table-centre cloth embroidered by my grandmother or a great-aunt. It will stay there as long as I live.

★★★

"Grieving for our mother is grieving for our childhood," wrote Albert Cohen. This sentence is stuck in my mind, going around and around in my head. A hole has formed in the hourglass of the present. I go a long way back, rediscover the dark-haired little girl I had left behind, the one with a peaceful childhood, the years adding up, the turkey at Christmas, the ham at Easter, and the St. Catherine's Day molasses candy my grandmother used to make. I recall the hours spent playing with my little brothers, the inexhaustible patience of my mother, and my grandfather's love.

My mother and father moved in with my grandparents after their marriage. The 1ère Avenue Nord house was my first home. We lived there until my younger brother was born. My parents were able to go out at night, put me to bed, leaving me in my grandfather's care. When they came home, I would be sitting on his knee, with him reading the newspapers to me, my mother said. "He woke you up, I'm sure he did." In one photo, he holds me in his arms, smiling. It is the only picture from that period in which he doesn't look sad. My aunt was ill, though. He was worried. I cheered him up, I made him feel glad to be alive again, it seems.

First transgression. I should be asleep, but I'm awake. I spend the evening in the comforting warmth of his body, in his tired-old-man smell, the quiet inflections of his voice. That's how I picture it, at least. To tell the truth, I have almost forgotten the tone of his voice, what he said, his gestures, his walk. But not his face or the food he prepared for my brothers and me, creating landscapes on our plates. Or our strolls together.

After my younger brother was born, he came to get me every day on 9ᵉ Avenue. He took me to Parc Victoria, showed me the plants, told me stories. My mother liked to remind me of it. How did she know since she stayed home? Perhaps she invented routes for us, conversations—the closeness she would have wanted with her father as a child. "He wore out two strollers taking you for walks," she used to say with a dreamy look in her eyes. When my mother was two, Léda became pregnant again. She must have tired easily as she was in delicate health. My aunt was born, then my grandmother had *the big operation*. A hysterectomy was risky in those days. The anxiety must have been palpable in the house. I am sure my mother felt it.

Léda survived. But she needed a long period of convalescence, and my mother was sent to Nicolet, to stay with Émilie, her maternal grandmother. She spent a whole year there. Had she found that year difficult? No, she hadn't been bored, she told me. In Nicolet were her aunts, her cousins, and there was liveliness and joy. She had gone to school even though she wasn't six yet. Her father sent her a lovely white dress and a veil for her first communion. She used to say, "my father," not "my parents."

"My father, your grandfather." How many times have I heard her say, "my father," while she didn't mention her mother much? Why was *he* the one who looked after me at night even though my grandmother was home? He was the centre of the family and Léda didn't mind, she idolized her husband. As did my mother, actually. As did I.

A memory. I must be four years old, we are in the garden behind the house. My mother wants to take a picture of us, her children, with her parents. I have a beautiful summer dress on, and little white boots. My brothers are wearing clean clothes. We're all in our Sunday best. We settle ourselves in front of the row of hollyhocks. She wants me to go and stand beside my grandmother, but I don't want to be near her, I want to be beside my grandfather.

I never learnt to love my grandmother. She didn't play with me or my brothers. She found us noisy. She kept telling us, "You'll be the death of your mother." She was sickly, nervous, had dizzy spells, never went out alone. Later, much later, I understood. They had removed her ovaries and womb at thirty-two years of age. They removed everything in those days and there were no replacement hormones.

I understood, but that didn't make me love her more. We, the children, didn't interest her. She preferred the company of grown-ups. My mother never felt the love for her that she had for her father. Her eyes didn't light up when her mother's image emerged, late at night, in the conversation. She would defend her, or excuse her, but she didn't show the affection that binds a child to one of its parents for life.

What would my mother have answered if I'd asked her if she'd loved Grandmother? She would have said she had. A daughter cannot admit that she didn't love the woman who brought her into the world—she would feel as though she were rejecting herself, doing away with herself. Unless the mother has been so harmful that one has to kill her within oneself in order to survive. Léda had nothing of the bad mother about her, she was a *goodenough mother*, defined by Winnicott as a woman who meets the needs of her child in a satisfactory way.

My mother respected her. She was proud that Léda had left to go to work in Drummondville, defying Émilie, her mother. Proud that she got married even though Émilie had spoken these terrible words, "Don't come and complain to me later." Léda was a rebel. Had she heard about feminism, which was in the air in North America in those years? In the kitchen on 1ère Avenue Nord, she occasionally mentioned that her brothers had completed their *cours classique* while the girls in the family had barely finished eighth or ninth grade. "That was the rule in those days," my mother would say to calm her down, but my grandmother didn't calm down. An injustice was an injustice. The girls had worked at home so the boys could get an education. And were their brothers grateful? I saw it the way Léda did. It infuriated me.

We may not love someone madly, yet still owe them our freedom. In the dormant town that was Sherbrooke at the time, Léda gave her daughters an avant-garde upbringing. Thanks to her, I had the same privileges as my brothers. I didn't have to fight to go to college or university. In photographs, Léda wears the facial expression of a strong, determined woman, stronger than my grandfather, as my mother always pointed out. *His* face is etched with sadness. His daughter's illness wears him down. He has been dying for a long time, he knows it, and I know it too. I cannot save him. My love won't be enough. Love cannot prevent death.

In the church where my family gathered to say goodbye to my grandfather with incense and prayers, I sat beside my younger brother. Next to us, my mother cried her eyes out. She could have controlled herself, adults shouldn't cry. I would remain stoic, I would know how to live with the death of my grandfather's love. I wouldn't shed a tear. I buried my early years without a tear. I would also bury my father and mother without a tear.

But even without tears, childhood hides away in a dark corner. It watches us. It never dies.

***

Words my mother spoke come back to me incessantly. They arise from the depths of oblivion and start dancing before me. Rambling conversations in the dimly lit living room while we watched the evening news, and monologues I would punctuate with a few distracted expressions of approval. My mother lived alone. For her, any visit was an opportunity to talk. I wish I could hear every single word of those conversations again, giving meaning to what had none for me then. With these small bits of memory, I strive to reassemble the jigsaw puzzle of a whole, now vanished, world.

Who was my grandmother Léda? And Émilie, her mother? When you say to your daughter, "get married if you want, but don't come and complain to me later," what are you talking about? Sexual relations, unbearable labour pains, housework? The inconsolable sorrow each time you lose a small child? When my mother repeated those words with a laugh, I would laugh along with her, thinking about Léda. It took courage for her to act against her mother's wishes, she must have been deeply in love. Or Émilie may not have been so unhappily married after all. This would be consistent with what my mother remembered. Émilie was a very capable woman! But that is all I know. And I barely know more about Léda, although we shared a bedroom for over ten years. In the past, that was enough for me, the family memory was stored in a certain place, my mother's brain. Now that place has been destroyed. I wander about in search of traces, with a nearly erased roadmap in my hands.

"If I had listened to my mother," Léda used to say, "I would never have made a life for myself." That is the lesson that has stayed with me. To have the audacity to go your own way. She came from a devout family. Both the eldest and the youngest girls had entered the congregation of the Soeurs grises. She slept under a large crucifix, said her rosary every day, made me say my morning and evening prayers. When she didn't have too many dizzy spells, she asked me to go to Mass with her. She believed in God. This is where her strength must have come from. It helped her live through her great ordeal, the illness of her daughter, a girl so beautiful and gifted in spite of it.

It all began on the threshold of adulthood. A nervous breakdown turning out badly, worsening problems, doctors, trips to Montreal for consultations, the psychiatrists at Allan Memorial and Dr. Cameron, wasted money, and an increasingly difficult situation. Since the grandparents had grown old, they could no longer look after their daughter. They had to make a decision. They had to admit her to the Saint-Michel-Archange hospital. They felt powerless, and guilty. "We had no choice anymore," my grandmother kept saying to convince herself. In her voice one could hear the pain that gnawed away at her day after day. My grandfather didn't survive my aunt's confinement.

I often asked my mother what was wrong with Lucienne, but she didn't know. Had she chosen to forget? She may have been schizophrenic but I never heard that word at home. They said she was ill, and that was that. Even today, mental illness remains a mystery. It was even more so in the thirties and forties. Psychiatry used barbaric means: straitjackets, electric shock treatments, lobotomy. Dr. Cameron had carried out strange experiments on his patients, my mother claimed.

Who was Donald Ewen Cameron? What I read about him sent shivers down my spine. Born in Scotland, he had emigrated to the United States and then settled in Montreal in 1943, where he became the director of the Royal Victoria Hospital's Allan Memorial Institute. So, my mother was right. By putting his patients into a state of prolonged sleep during which they were made to listen to tapes, Dr. Cameron wanted to re-program them. These brainwashing experiments were later funded by the C.I.A. LSD was used, as well. When all this became known after Dr. Cameron's death, several patients registered complaints.

Had Dr. Cameron already introduced his methods when my

aunt was being treated? There is no way of knowing. My aunt's file has long since been destroyed. The people who treated her have died. And if I learnt the truth, where would it get me? What matters to me is an understanding of what my aunt's illness changed for us. For my mother, my grandparents, my father, and us, the children. *Illness*, how many times did I hear that word at home? Madness was never spoken of. We were taught to regard our aunt with respect, she was ill, as though she suffered from tuberculosis or diabetes. And the neighbours had no choice but to regard her with respect as well. I didn't grasp how forward-thinking this view really was.

A memory. I am eight or nine. We are going to see our aunt at Saint-Michel-Archange with an uncle on my father's side. My grandmother stays at home; she doesn't feel up to coming. It's a long way, but my uncle has bought a beautiful Mercury. We are happy, and my aunt is happy to see us too. I barely recognize her. Her hair is completely white, and she has a funny white dress on, she looks funny and she says funny things. My mother thinks it's because of the medication. There are many other patients, and they look funny too. I don't budge from my chair, but I look all around me. I wouldn't like to live here. My mother is reassured, though. The nuns are kind, they give my aunt the parcels we send her, so we don't need to worry. We won't need to worry anymore. "Lucienne doesn't look unhappy," my mother repeated that evening, "she is well treated." And my grandmother responded with a radiant voice.

I instantly recognized the façade of the Saint-Michel-Archange hospital in Denise Filiatrault's film about Alys Robi. A fabulous career, followed by a descent into hell. Nervous breakdown, hospitalization, insulin treatments, electroconvulsive therapy, lobotomy. At the end of the screening, I tried to hide my reddened eyes. I was probably the only member of the audience to have set foot in the hospital where Alys Robi ended up. Around me, people discussed the film, they criticized the psychiatry of those years, recalling hazy memories of the singer. Really, what a talent, but what a way for her life to end! And I, I thought about my aunt, working out the dates in my head. At the time of her hospitalization, in 1954, neuroleptic drugs were already being prescribed. She had escaped the barbarity. That's what I want to believe, anyway.

A few months later, a television report on psychiatric hospitals was announced. I called my mother to let her know. She wasn't going to watch the program. She told me straightaway that she couldn't. I hadn't realized until then just how hard that period had been for her. She always avoided letting us know that. Certain scenes came back to me like forgotten ghosts. I am quietly playing on the living room carpet while the adults talk among themselves. My grandfather says that my aunt is acting strangely; she gets angry and she goes out in her dressing gown. He doesn't know what to do anymore. Later, I will also hear new words: *tranquillizer, ambulance, hospital*. My aunt is confined to a mental hospital in Quebec City. My grandfather is upset. My grandmother is upset. My mother doesn't say how she feels. She tries to reason with her parents, that's all she can do for them.

In the early sixties, thanks to new drugs, my aunt began to feel better. Cheerful, well-dressed, she was allowed to spend a few days at home. My grandmother rejoiced. She never thought she would be blessed with seeing her again. Then came the period of de-institutionalization. Those in charge asked the family to welcome her back. They insisted. And my parents agreed, which couldn't have been easy for them. Lucienne was functional, as they say nowadays, but she had odd whims, sudden changes of mood, and somewhat paranoid ideas. Fortunately, she eventually went to live in an apartment. My mother didn't drop her, however. She was big sister to the end. We expected she would not die as long as Lucienne was alive, and we were right.

If Lucienne had been *my* sister, she could almost certainly have been treated. Or her condition improved, at least. But don't we have great difficulty understanding even today how the brain works? Not enough has been said about the anguish of families dealing with mental illness day after day.

★★★

When I was a child, I wanted to become a pianist like my mother, like my great-aunts and my great-grandmother, Octavie, who composed melancholy waltzes. But there was no money for music lessons. "I'll teach you myself," my mother told me. She found time, she had studied music for eight or nine years. I spent long hours at the out-of-tune piano my grandfather had bought for his daughters. I practised my scales, I learnt to read notes and play short pieces by Beethoven and Brahms from tattered books. One day, I stopped. I was no longer making progress. My mother didn't force me to practise. And the old piano had more and more false notes.

Yet my mother could make it resonate. On Sunday afternoons, in her clean dress and sometimes a pearl necklace, she got out her music books and ran her fingers, which smelled of bleach, over the keyboard. This image is still clear: my grandmother in her armchair, a cup of tea in her hand, is listening to my mother with a smile on her face while I sit on the sofa. I gaze up at Degas's dancers, looking so elegant in the frame above the piano. Then I lower my eyes, watch my mother concentrating on the notes in her music book. I am proud of her. She is so beautiful in her Sunday dress. We may not have a bungalow, but my mother can play the piano.

Music showed that we were cultured. And when you are cultured, you have class. Until the end of her life, my mother liked to tell me an anecdote. My grandfather had accompanied an aunt to Montreal, to Archambault, where she wanted to buy some scores. She was badly dressed. The saleswomen made fun of her when she asked for a particularly difficult piece. Was she aware of the disdain? She sat down at the piano, began to play. Everyone in the store, customers, saleswomen, the manager, drew near to listen to her. Clothes don't make the man, that's what my mother wanted to instill in me, just as her father instilled it in her. As a tailor, he knew exactly what that saying meant.

The piano followed my mother to the apartment on rue Bowen after my father died, as did Degas's dancers in their yellowing tutus. She never opened it again, or hardly ever, she was afraid to disturb the neighbours and she suffered from arthritis. She would spread out her hands in the evening when I came to see her, show me her crooked fingers. But she had good eyes, and the resonance of words replaced that of music. She could read for hours on end in the dimly lit living room—books we brought her, biographies, memoirs, novels. And Proust, whom she devoured, both fascinated and annoyed her, as though it were a soap opera. "All those rich, temperamental people. I would rather get the maid's point of view," she said. She pitied Françoise having to wait on them day after day.

For a long time, I thought that at every visit of Marcel to the Duchesse de Guermantes, at every gathering at the Verdurins, my mother relived the hardships of our childhood: the counting and recounting of the pennies to try and make ends meet, the wealth of ingenuity she needed to deploy, and the strenuous work of making things shine that didn't shine. I also knew how much she admired Jean Lesage, who had made it possible for us to get an education, and her love for René Lévesque—hadn't he given us back our electricity? The Quiet Revolution was a golden age for her. She believed in it as if it were a religion.

Yet there was something else, which she concealed or denied. Something I tried to grasp, but couldn't, whenever we rehashed the family stories. One evening, a few years before she died, it slipped out, I don't remember how. We were talking once again about my grandfather. She started to go back in time to before I was born, before she was married, and before her years in Toronto. She lived in the family home. It was the early forties. And I heard, "Your grandfather wasn't like other people." She had told me a hundred times that he didn't go to Mass on Sunday—my mother's friends still reminded her of that when they came to see her—so I expected it to be mentioned yet again, but I was startled by the revelation that, "he had communist sympathies." Then, because she had got carried away, she quickly added to reassure me, "but he wasn't a member of the Party."

A whole chapter of the past resurfaced at once—the catechism classes in primary school, the nuns telling us about the horrors of communism in Russia, Catholics being tortured because they refused to trample on the crucifix, a barbarity similar to that of the Indians martyring our good missionaries. And my fear, my fear that the Russians might unleash a war, that they'd come all the way to where we were, to Sherbrooke, where we lived in peace with the Protestants in their tiny churches. *They*, at least, had never thought of torturing us.

My mother couldn't make that revelation when I was a child, since it had to be kept from people at school. But why wait so long? Was she ashamed of her own father's political position? She wasn't, because she too stood up for the destitute. She continued to protect her father even in the Duplessis years. I asked her how people behaved in Sherbrooke in those days when someone had communist sympathies. My grandfather's friends used to come to the house, my mother said. They talked among themselves, but as soon as they went out again, they fell silent. Between indoors and the outside world was a clear, impervious, impassable barrier.

I picture the living room of the house where I was raised, on 1ère Avenue Nord: the wine red corduroy sofa, the piano, the Persian carpet. Everything is new, there are no signs yet of wear and tear from the passing years. It's evening, a fall or winter evening, and three or four men have got together. They're reading passages —Marx, Engels—and they talk among themselves. My mother, I'm sure, is eavesdropping on them. What did she remember? She never told us. But after my father died, she began to read Marx and Mao in her new apartment.

Only a few sentences of that time still linger in my mind, "Your grandfather didn't practise his beliefs. He published stories in the newspaper with a friend." Or, "He had thought of emigrating to Argentina." He must have found Quebec terribly narrow, he longed to be in a different milieu. He had lived in New York and then in Winnipeg. He was getting ready to travel around the world when he met my grandmother, he would have been capable of leaving everything. But he didn't take his family off to a foreign country, he stayed in Sherbrooke. For the sake of his wife, his two daughters? The language? Or the unsurmountable difficulties he sensed? It's a mystery. And would my mother have wanted to head off to the ends of the earth? I never thought of asking her. Why didn't I? That's the *real* mystery.

I am weaving my threads out of nothing. I collect and I interpret. I trim this nothing with the fierce will to salvage the past. This narrative is a fabric full of holes in which I try to capture my mother. I would like her to have no more secrets for us. Yet she resists me, as if to say, "Don't try to immobilize me, it won't work." And I see before me, in black and white, the outline of my defeat. I know I am tangled up in my own fiction. My mother has become a character in a novel, so has my grandfather, and grandmother, and my aunt. I am facing an ever shakier reality. I wanted to be with them again, all of them, as in the days of 1ère Avenue Nord, but every sentence I write carries me a little farther away from them.

And what if I was deluding myself? What if my narrative was prompted by a hidden desire to distort my childhood, to turn it into a suitable story, with causes and effects, a beginning and an end? A childhood that no longer rebels, a quietened-down childhood, relegated to an album I can open and close again as I please when a gloomy mood comes over me. Writing that can imprison the past, stop the ghosts from returning whenever they choose. And I, free at last to change, to become an unattached woman, to emigrate to countries with unfamiliar languages without feeling guilty for abandoning my dead.

★★★

We slowly grow used to an absence. It happens quietly, unintentionally. I didn't think of calling my mother yesterday when on television they announced the transit of Venus across the Sun. I only felt a twinge of sadness. She used to gaze at the stars from the glass doors of her living room. Who did she get that passion for astronomy from? At night, on the telephone, I would listen with half an ear to her talking about Mars or Jupiter, my mind on the next day's work. I didn't make time to take an interest in what interested her. With my daughter and grandson, I do.

"We always love our children more than our mother." She is the one who blurted out that phrase many years ago, no doubt because she preferred us, the three of us, to her own mother. I have never forgotten that moment. She gave me permission to love my daughter more than her. She always accepted that my brothers and I gave precedence to our children over her. She wasn't demanding or temperamental with us, unlike many other aging parents. But did she prefer her children to her father? What would she have said if I had asked her that?

Why didn't I ask her more questions? I must have known I wouldn't get any answers. Was it because she refused to admit things to herself that she didn't want to see? Or was she guarding her secrets? One evening, she said to me that a woman didn't have to tell her children everything. That lesson stayed with me. Deep down I agreed with her. Did I really need to know if my father had been her first lover? Because, in the end, the big question a daughter longs to ask her mother is the one about love.

My mother had enjoyed making love. She admitted it in veiled terms when, to cheer her up, I would ask her at night on the telephone if she was getting dressed to go bar-hopping to meet a man. "I wouldn't feel like it anymore, now" she would answer back right away with a burst of laughter. The word *now* said it all. I could see her again in the kitchen on 1ère Avenue Nord. My father was coming home from work, he headed straight towards her and put his arms around her hips. She would laugh, a kind of laugh I couldn't decode. I understood a few years later, when blood appeared between my thighs.

How would I have reacted if she had remarried after my father died? The idea had never occurred to me. Like her friends, she faced her widowhood without grumbling, poked fun at the women in her building who were looking for a partner. She enjoyed living alone, not having to make concessions, no explanations. She could eat when it suited her, read late at night. She was too old for desire but didn't want to discuss that with me.

She was a woman of her generation. I knew nothing of the mysteries of life when I called her to come to the bathroom one evening in March, shortly before my twelfth birthday. Panic-stricken, I had just seen that my panties were covered in blood. My mother came upstairs, took a quick look and, without flinching, explained it all to me in clinical terms, then ended with, "Just put it out of your mind." Of course, it was all I could think of for months on end. Mating was so revolting! How could you call that *love*? What a sacrifice you needed to make so you could have children! My mother and I never spoke about it again. Was it modesty? Did she feel uneasy about sexuality? I just don't know, nor do I understand why I never tried to bring it up with her.

In my memory, two women face each other. In a cold voice, one explains life to me as a fate striking women since the world began, and the other admits on the phone with a laugh that she really doesn't feel like it anymore. I used to wonder which mother was mine. Eventually I understood. It was the same woman at two different times in history: during the Duplessis era, and when that fresh wind swept across Quebec in the Quiet Revolution, making my mother happy to be alive.

★★★

I'd been waiting for this moment for six whole months. Finally, last night, for the first time, my mother came back to me. She looked like one of those plump storybook fairies leaning over a cradle. She arrived at my door with her walker, all smiles. I was happy to see her again. She hadn't abandoned us for good, then. But my heart started pounding right away. How would I manage to get everything done? I still had that heavy workload in spite of my retirement and, of course, *life*: the house, day-to-day matters to settle, the mail. And my grandson whom I would have to leave, as I needed to last fall. But I held out my arms to her. I calmed down.

Last November's anxiety had resurfaced. My life had never felt so burdensome to me. This life of a modern woman, which I had wanted nonetheless with an unflinching determination, left no room for illness or death. Fortunately, I no longer taught. How could I have coped if on the day of my mother's cardiovascular incident I would have been in the middle of term? When my grandson was born prematurely, near the end of the academic year, it had distressed me that I could not fully enjoy his arrival. The question came up again when my mother's health deteriorated. How much space are we allowed to give to life's major events?

When I woke up, I wondered why the mother in that dream wasn't the mother of my childhood: beautiful, young, and spirited, as I most often imagined her. Did she want to check if I was ready to see her come back to life? If I was able now to sacrifice everything for her, even though I tried to find an assisted-living residence for her last fall? I felt guilt about not having done enough. It's no use reasoning with yourself, blaming oneself after a death is part of mourning.

It's been six months now since my mother died, six months, and my mourning isn't proceeding the way it does in books. Nowadays, you are supposed to get on with it, as with your daily tasks. You must quickly put your sorrow away in a cupboard. If you have the audacity to admit a few weeks after the funeral that you are distraught, you will be looked upon as someone who can't overcome hardships. And in a world that turns at the speed of light, what woman wants to show her fragility? It's better to keep quiet. Better to endure the loss alone, or with a few friends who have been faced with death too.

People used to wear mourning clothes. *Porter le deuil,* the way you carry a heavy load on your shoulders, a weight that bends you down. I can still see my grandmother in black after the death of her husband. Black dress, black hat, black veil, black gloves. For a year, that is how she dressed whenever she went out. Later, she replaced black with grey, violet, and white. Two years for a bereavement, that was the custom, no one worried about her ability to deal with her grief. Today, people would advise her to see a therapist.

My father's death didn't confront me with such a cruel truth. It was late spring. Courses were finished, so I didn't have to turn up in front of a class every day. I had asked for educational leave and I was getting ready to move to Montreal. I would begin a doctoral program in September, I was thirty-one, with a new life ahead of me. And my mother was very much alive, she would be old when she died, very old, like my great-grandmother Émilie. And so would I. I still had two thirds of the way to go.

It was later that I felt the threat. When the first friends began to weaken. What did the future hold for me, I wondered? But loneliness settled within me for good in the hospital room where, with each sigh, my mother drew closer to the abyss. I couldn't do anything for her, nor could my brothers, her grandchildren, the nurses, or the doctor. She had sunk into a sleep where no one could reach her. She was preparing herself for the respiratory distress. The great duel was about to begin, and we would be mere spectators. She would be hopelessly alone. And so would I. If I asked for a double dose of morphine earlier that evening, it was because I felt utterly helpless seeing her in such pain. What can you do to bring relief to your mother? Helpless and lonely were overlapping words. I had often become annoyed when I heard the phrase, "We are born alone and we die alone." It wasn't a cliché anymore.

How long ago did my mother enter her final loneliness? Perhaps that is why she didn't prepare us for her death. Her children should remain on the side of life. I can still hear her voice, one fall evening, in the dimly lit living room. A neighbour of hers had lost her husband. The poor woman had gone into a depression, and my mother blurted out to me, "One has got to pull oneself together," just as she used to tell me, "We shouldn't pay too much attention to our feelings." Why exactly shouldn't we pay attention to our feelings? Yet my mother had gone through a difficult time herself after my father died. Perhaps she had been afraid she might go under. Thankfully, she had pulled herself together. I wonder how she had found the strength. Where is the dividing line between a memory we have come to terms with and one that might carry us off?

We think we have grown used to someone's absence, but all it takes is a dream to confront us once again with the naked truth of death.

***

We shouldn't pay too much attention to our feelings. Should we refuse to listen to the small voice that whispers in our ear to take care of ourselves? Or, just the opposite, refuse to let ourselves sink into despair? I am not sure I fully grasp what my mother meant. But she was talking about pain and women. This I know. There were so many women in Quebec at that time who paid no attention to their feelings. The edict came to them from the distant past, from immigrating into an icy country, from the terrible life during colonization, from scurvy, wars, the defeat, from having to reproduce in order to ensure the survival of French Canada. It came to them from grandmothers who gave birth every year and those who died from it.

Louisa, that grandmother I never met, died following *the big operation* in 1911, after bringing five sons into the world. She wasn't as fortunate as Léda, who had the operation in 1918 or 1919. And Émilie, Léda's mother, survived fifteen deliveries, but endured hellish labour pains each time. It took two men to hold her down. What kind of help could they possibly give her? Did they stop her from throwing herself out of the window?

Octavie, my grandfather's mother, had seventeen children in sixteen years, without a single set of twins. When the parish priest asked my great-grandmother as he gave her the last rites if she was afraid of death, she answered, "Father, I have seen death seventeen times." Pensively, my mother would say, "childbirth in those days, you know." No ultrasounds, no epidurals, no relief. And many children didn't reach the age of six. None of Octavie's daughters got married and, among her four granddaughters, only my mother had a man in her life. Is that so surprising? My brothers and I are Octavie's only descendants. It would seem that my mother's desire to have children was stronger than fear. I wonder if she got that from Léda's side of the family.

"You shall give birth in pain," the priest declared from the pulpit on Sunday, in the same voice as when he said, "You shall not kill." For men to reach the point of ascribing such a commandment to their God, they must have been terrified by the suffering of women in labour. It had to be a punishment. The daughters of Eve needed to atone for the sin of their ancestress, the woman by whom misfortune was brought into the world. Since the beginning of time, pain has been women's business, something passed on from mother to daughter. We can imagine the subconscious guilt of mothers of newborns when, after hours and hours of torture, a girl was laid in their arms, condemned like them to pain. And their relief when they were told, "It's a boy."

On the eve of her death, Octavie had rebelled. She wanted to remind the priest that he should have kept quiet, for she knew more about the great passage than he did. She knew what he was ignorant of, he who hadn't had to fight seventeen times against death. My mother quoted Octavie's words to me on numerous occasions, but only after I decided not to have any more children, to avoid instilling fear in me. Perhaps that is also why she always vehemently denied having had labour pains herself.

Contrary to all expectations, reality caught up with her on the evening of December 30th, 2011. She was lifted up by great waves of pain, which would subside only to return at once, great waves like those of a woman in labour. She was giving birth but, this time, to her own death. I didn't send for the priest. I simply asked for morphine.

★★★

My mother was thirty-five when she became my mother. I shall never know who she was before, but I accept that now. I don't need to know everything. I can leave gaps and patches of darkness, I can even show contradictions. When a woman lives to be a hundred or almost, her face will change along with the times.

I wasn't very interested. I didn't ask my mother many questions about her life. I preferred to let her talk, in the evening, about whatever she was willing to reveal. Shyness? Tact? Fear, rather, of getting no for an answer. I couldn't have borne it. It would have been too painful to feel separated from her or worse, rejected. The slight difference between the words *separation* and *rejection* is something I've never actually understood. My mother spun a thick cocoon around her children that held us in its warmth. Breaking the cocoon meant experiencing banishment, exile.

For me, that cocoon takes on the image of the family home, where we went to live when we returned to Sherbrooke. I was two when I left it, and seven when I came back. I would live there until I was twenty. A large house with many windows, two storeys, a basement, and an attic we were forbidden to set foot in. I can still clearly see my grandmother's bedroom, where I slept too. My brothers had the room at the back, the one that opened onto the balcony. At the time, one didn't know what it meant to have a room of one's own. Families had several children and they often included the old parents. The bathroom was the only room where you could be alone. No one complained about the lack of privacy.

I see the house as a net covering us with a love that couldn't unravel—us, the children, merged into a single picture. Same wants, same needs, same schedule, same meals, the same constant care. It was impossible to escape or get into mischief. Not because we feared punishment, but because we were afraid to upset a mother who devoted all her time—all her dreams—to us. We were a generation of dutiful children. We understood very early what we owed our mothers. We were their pride, their success, their goal in life. These mothers didn't want us to leave them. And mine was no exception. She wished to keep us within her tender sphere, she enveloped us. Hadn't she brought us into the world at an age when her friends already had teenagers? She must have been terribly scared she would never have children. Fortunately, she met my father.

A woman should help her children break away from her as early as possible. She should both love her little ones unconditionally and throw them out of the nest. Isn't that demanding the impossible? We do what we can, with our abilities, our past, our wounds. As time passed, I stopped asking perfection of my mother. It was up to me to find the strength to move away. And, for that, endure the misery of guilt. Daughters feel they are never doing enough for their mother, like mothers for their children. The bond with the mother is a knot we never untie, never completely untie. We will have to live with suffering that embeds itself in our flesh, that turns into physical pain. Guilt is perverse, it seeps in without us being aware of it, and settles in the pit of the stomach. We only have to hear, "I waited all night for your phone call," or "When are you coming to see me?" to become the little girl again who upsets her mother, and we sleep badly. We think we are neglecting our mother when we don't satisfy her every whim.

Men feel guilty, too. But it seems to me that mothers are less demanding of their sons than of their daughters. Women have been brought up to look after others and feminism hasn't penetrated to the very core of our being. Can it be any other way in the face of behaviour passed down for thousands of years? We are at a turning point in our civilization, but it's easier to get used to social media than to transform the mother-daughter relationship. A great sacrifice is demanded from a mother to agree to her daughter moving away from her. And it takes great courage for a daughter to live with a poor image of herself if she separates from her mother.

I have always surrounded myself with friends, projects, books, objects, activities, and cats. Perhaps it has been to recreate the cocoon elsewhere, to escape the immense sadness of loneliness. Separation from the beloved mother, loneliness, insurmountable sadness. Dreaming of being back in the warmth of that great love. Have mothers, who gave themselves body and soul to their children, placed them in the path of inescapable melancholy?

★★★

Perhaps this narrative is a fraud. Worse, a betrayal. I just wrote that my mother spun an indestructible cocoon around her children. Yet, she encouraged us in our studies, and she never put a damper on our love affairs, our projects, or our travels. We left home at a very young age, leaving Sherbrooke without remorse. We never returned except for short visits.

I went to see my mother regularly, as did my brothers. She lived for our visits. We could hear it in her voice when we told her we were coming. Her happy years were back. What would she cook for us? Roast beef, a meat loaf, shepherd's pie? And for dessert, apple pie, date squares or a jelly roll? Like all mothers, she knew what our favourite dishes were, she wanted to please us. The older she got, the longer it took her to get ready. She had to shop, do the housework, make the bed if we slept there and, of course, cook the meals. I kept telling her, "Don't go to so much trouble," but it was no use. Then I no longer said anything. Our visits kept her busy for more than a week. I understood. If you are ninety years old, you don't get much done in a day.

    She wouldn't see anyone on the days before our visits. One of her friends told me that my mother abandoned her as soon as we let her know we were coming. "Mme C. called and asked me to go out with her, but I can't spare the time." I would gently scold her, she shouldn't give up her friends, we could cook together, but it was no good. She was happy, as when we were small, when we needed her. One evening, when she was going to repair one of my skirts, I protested a little more than usual, I suppose. She replied, "I want to feel useful. When you'll be my age, you'll understand." I kept quiet after that. I let her cook for me, sew up the hems of my skirts or dresses, knit socks for me, so cozy in winter boots. I even bought wool for her. "It's good for my fingers," she'd explain.

    Loving us, waiting for us, pampering us was her life. She was a mother with a capital M, supreme, complete, like so many other women. Like Albert Cohen's mother, who went as far as becoming enslaved to her beloved son. After her death, he realized that no woman would ever show such perfect self-denial to him. "My mother didn't have a self, but a son," he wrote. I was outraged. How could he be delighted about that, enjoy it even? It is a son's statement, not a daughter's. Women don't feel such passion for their daughters. The daughters wouldn't be able to bear it anyway, they would soon feel smothered, swallowed up.

    One day, when I visited her, my mother announced she had a meeting of her group, she would like to go. I encouraged her right away, I had work to do, what a good idea! I felt reassured—she wasn't living only for us, her children. She had just read Simone de Beauvoir, and was becoming liberated. Although I couldn't come as often as I would have wished, I now knew that she liked to see her friends. It wasn't just to fill the time when we weren't there. I went back to Montreal the next day feeling lighter. But she must have blamed herself, she never again left the house during one of my visits. She had gone back to her role as the perfect mother. How could I have thought that at over seventy years of age, she could step out of it so easily?

For me, my mother will always be a woman of contradictions. Unlike Albert Cohen's mother, she was fond of literature and the arts. She was interested in politics, history, geography, anthropology, and astronomy. After my father died, I suggested she enroll in the senior citizen university, but she refused. It was out of the question—it didn't appeal to her. I was disappointed. How could a woman who had encouraged our studies so much, ignore this opportunity to broaden her knowledge? Later, I understood. The older she got, the more difficult it became for her to leave her apartment, even to come and stay for a few days with her children. Her world had shrunk.

I guessed the senior citizen university was also a question of money to her. "We don't know what tomorrow will bring, we have to be careful," she'd say. Economize, count every penny, that's what she had been doing for fifty years. When you have got out of the habit of treating yourself, can you really go back to your old ways? She would rather save her money for us. She gave us presents on every one of our birthdays, took her grandchildren to the movies or a restaurant.

Once in a while, in the evening, in the dimly lit living room, I reminded her that she should take advantage of the little money she and my father had saved. They had given all three of us an education, and we earned a good living. But she wouldn't hear of it. "I am happy," she said, "what do you want me to buy for myself?" If I argued, she would eventually admit, "When I die, I would like to leave you something." Then I gave up. She had the last word, as always. I too often let her have the last word. I should have persisted, but I didn't go to see her to have our talk end with a quarrel. I had come to please her.

Entrenched in her own point of view, she didn't see that I would have been thrilled to spoil her a little by paying for a taxi to go to the Carrefour de l'Estrie shopping centre when she couldn't take the bus anymore, or by taking her out to a restaurant. She refused point blank, she wanted to stay home. It was no use insisting. Later, I began to order meals in, which was my little victory. She went along with it, and I often managed to pay the delivery man before she could open her wallet. Then, one day, at noon, she didn't protest. She had given up, she surrendered to her fate, it was no longer important for her to remain in control. I realized she had just entered extreme old age, and my eyes filled with tears. I would rather she had stubbornly refused, as usual.

★★★

It's so hot out that I would welcome a heavy snowfall. At this time in previous years, my mother complained about the scorching heat in every one of our phone calls. Then she'd start laughing, "We are never satisfied." The vagaries of the weather punctuated her life. In the winter she was afraid she might fall, break a hip. Ice often covered the sidewalks until Easter. In the fall, it was the rain. She went out less and less often. Going out meant going for her walk in the park, near the Rivière Saint-François. She would lovingly look at the trees, admiring them. In summer she walked with her head down in search of four-leaf clovers. I found several in books I lent her. She also gave me some. "They'll bring you luck." She had her little superstitions. I would carefully take the clovers in my hands and, being briefly superstitious too, put them in a book.

No more four-leaf clovers this summer, no more walks, and no more conversations about the unbearable heat in her apartment. My brother had put in an air conditioner, but she was afraid to have it on at night or when she went down to the dining room. "You never know." What could possibly have happened? It was useless to try and reason with her. My mother's stubbornness annoyed me. Now, it moves me. We see things differently after death. In their fears, old people are like children imagining there are monsters under their beds. Actually, I didn't want to consider my mother an old woman. She had accustomed us to seeing her as still young and spirited. And I saw her as young and spirited until the final weeks of her life. She managed to fool me.

But I am simplifying. When exactly are people no longer capable of making decisions for themselves? We notice a lapse of memory, then a second one, and a third, then a slowing of the gait as it becomes less and less steady. The signs pile up but we choose to ignore them. One day, we face the facts: our mother cannot live alone much longer. We telephone the local community services centre, we explain, and ask for advice. Someone tells us that a social worker will come to assess the situation. With pounding heart, we put down the receiver.

I remember the social worker's visit down to the last detail. The grey November afternoon, the trees bending in the wind, the woman's arrival, in a neutral coat, neutral blouse, and neutral pants. A kind, conscientious woman. She asks questions, filling out her form. And my mother, upright in her easy chair, who tries to pull the wool over the woman's eyes, assures her that she goes for a walk in the park every day, goes down to the dining room of the residence every day. The woman looks at me, and I, stunned, discreetly shake my head, no, not anymore. Is she lying? Or is she living in the past? She is saving her skin, she doesn't want to leave her apartment.

The woman insists, and my mother resists her. Mustering her last resources, she shows her she can still sit down on the toilet, lie down, and get up without any problem. She has regained her abilities, and I look like an ungrateful daughter who wants to get rid of her mother, and I feel hopelessly sad while my mother struggles like a cat someone is trying to put into a cage to take it to the SPCA. The social worker tests the waters; suggests she might go to a convalescent home for a while, and my mother firmly answers no. So we will have to force her to leave. In the window, the grey November sky hangs so heavy it seems about to fall.

After sadness and guilt came aggressiveness. Why wasn't my mother aware of the situation? Why leave the horrible decision to us, her children, whom she said she loved more than anything? She wasn't alone, though. So many friends had described similar scenes to me. Before them, people didn't end their days in a nursing home. And *we* would have models, we would know how to take the necessary decisions and not have our children bear the full weight. But how could we foresee what we would become in a few decades? Instinct, what we really want, feelings: these are much more powerful than experience gained. I couldn't claim the moral high ground.

I needed to act, though. I needed to assume the role of ungrateful daughter, initiate a procedure while hoping for a miracle. But there was no miracle, and I had to get used to an image of myself as a daughter unwilling to sacrifice everything so her mother could stay in her apartment. It is pointless to reason with ourselves, to tell ourselves that life doesn't demand such a sacrifice from a child, that our mother wouldn't have wanted it either. Yet, in the end, we have to accept the truth. Whether we admit it or not, uprooting one's mother at ninety-seven years of age is an act of unbelievable violence.

Violence is splashed across our screens in the coverage of wars, in the slaughter inside movie theatres or universities. But we no longer see it beneath the small, tight clothes of everyday life. A child going hungry, a woman afraid of her husband, a man so old he can't go on. There are organizations, social services, and residences with smiling old people holding hands during the commercials. There are those nursing homes politicians visit during election campaigns. No one dares to ask if some of the living-dead are still able to vote. The politicians pretend to listen to them, they add up the billions, subtract, divide. They forget the distress or, rather, put it to sleep.

Growing old is getting used to violence. The body no longer following, the mind misfiring, the daily tasks becoming more and more difficult. Other people not understanding, and wanting the best for us. It is seeing our children as enemies. It is living a life of pain.

★★★

"And I awake and I am terror-stricken by my solitude." I endlessly repeat Albert Cohen's words to myself. They have entrenched themselves in my flesh. What ghost emerges from my mother's death, what monstrous reality threatens me? My own death suddenly waiting in the shadows? No, that would be too simple. Death, rather, with a capital D, timeless, death as a supreme violence capable of destroying everything, of making sure nothing survives us. Neither children, nor grandchildren, students, parents, or friends. Neither cities, nor countries, or books. Nothing and no one. Every time, the mother's death is a revelation that all will end one day. Every time, it is an apocalypse.

The terror also struck a small boy, bewildered at seeing his great-grandmother being put into a hole, then left there, one snowy, blustery morning. The world plunged into dread for him, and I had to find acceptable words. "Grandma's body is asleep in the coffin, at the cemetery, but her soul is now in heaven above, with that grandpa whose picture I showed you in the album from the filing cabinet." Heaven is beautiful, it's huge, and Grandma is happy. "Can you play catch there?" the little boy asked. Of course, I'm sure Grandma plays catch with Grandpa every day. He smiled, reassured. He could go back to what he was doing. Religion is the only consolation possible. The need for it is understandable.

At three years of age, my father lost his parents. Toussaint, his father, fell off the roof of his house while clearing it of snow. And Louisa died as well, after her operation. What questions had this disaster left lingering in his mind, what images? He was too small to understand the workings of heaven, but it may have been what took his breath away for as long as he lived. "Asthma is no joke," Mama used to say. Suddenly, for no reason, Papa would gasp for air, he'd turn completely red, take his puffer, and we had to call the doctor. Would he arrive in time? Terror shook the house. Death appeared to us, it loomed before us like a Halloween ghost. Wasn't my father born on October 31st?

Once the terror had passed, life resumed, as did our games, and the story my mother read to us in the clean bed. We'd fall asleep with images of happy princesses who had lots of children, and whose princes didn't suffer from asthma. I don't know what surfaced in my sleep, the dread of death or the certainty I would reach the age of a hundred. Because in my mother's family people lived to nearly a hundred, as she told us again and again, perhaps to ease her mind. Despite the inevitable bereavements, death didn't succeed in building its nest in our home. My mother chased it away. Life prevailed.

With a little luck, I will see the next thirty years. But who can guarantee it? Around me, so many people my age have already died—sudden cancers, heart attacks, accidents, suicides. Death appears in many guises. But it wasn't until my mother's last weeks that I learnt to say, "I am mortal." Mortal, yes, and all the more alive. Until the very end, my mother's eyes gazed with wonder at the morning light, the afternoon sun, and the impenetrable darkness of night gathering earlier and earlier. Then, she would gaze at the dome of what used to be the Saint-Vincent hospital, which would suddenly light up as in a *son et lumière* spectacle. I'd suggest we have a glass of wine, she'd agree with a laugh, and the evening was off to a joyful start. Who cared what tomorrow would bring?

For now, there was a good meal, television programs, and phone calls from her sons. Afterwards we'd play our game of solitaire together, as she'd been doing every night for decades. What I had called until then her *denial*, didn't seem a simple defense mechanism anymore. It struck me that it sprang from her very strength, from an ability to forget about the looming threat in order to enjoy life's final days. Could denial be a philosophy, a talent for happiness? What should we call it then? What can we call the ability to stop the terror of death from engulfing us?

No one could have known that the woman who quietly sipped her aperitif with me would be at death's door a week from then. Later, a friend from the health network told me, "Had I known she was so close to death, I would never have recommended a geriatric assessment." Had we known, would we have made the decisions we made? We would most certainly have let my mother end her days in her apartment. Her love of life managed to fool us all. To the end.

★★★

In the air hangs a smell of moldy, decaying leaves too heavy to whirl up in the icy wind. Soon it will snow. We are shivering, my family and I. We hold chrysanthemums we have come to place against the gravestone in front of the name Cécile P., carved under my father's name. I stand above my mother's coffin. She must be a pile of putrid flesh by now. In what condition is a dead body after ten months? I try to see it in my mind's eye. A waste of time.

Why can't I picture her in a state of decomposition? I never wondered about such a thing after my father died. When he was buried here, I was a young woman with plans, problems, a young woman's dreams. Death only worried me in a vague way, it would go and build its nest in a body that was already tired, an uncle's or an aunt's. Now it may settle in mine.

I had got used to seeing my mother as a woman on her own. Here, she is reunited with my father, as in the snapshots of my album, where she beams her loveliest smile at the camera, happy to be beside her man and three children. She is wearing her Sunday dress, a sleeveless one, a bit low-cut. She shows her fine skin, her firm arms. She must be a little over forty. Summertime, the garden, the hollyhock hedge, these fragrances I would still recognize with my eyes closed, as I would my mother's perfume. It was a good-quality perfume she kept for special occasions. But in our family there *were* no special occasions, so it stayed in its bottle. Some Sundays my mother took it out and sprayed two or three drops on my wrists. I didn't wash myself on those nights, I knew I was my mother's daughter.

She hated the cheap perfumes neighbours splashed on themselves, the smell often mixing with that of hair spray. It turned her stomach at Sunday Mass, she wasn't sure she would be able to receive communion. I agreed with her, but I cheated a little. I would stop for a moment to look at the bottles on dime-store shelves. There were some pretty ones in velvet cases. But I didn't buy any. I didn't give my mother any. I didn't wear perfume.

Even today, I don't wear any. Yet I have gone to department stores, airport shops, Parisian perfumeries, and cosmetics shelves in drugstores. I have been splashed, given advice to, encouraged to buy some brand or other. I never did buy any. It's as though at the bottom of the bottle there is always a funeral-parlour smell, and I would rather leave it slumbering there, like those malevolent spirits one shouldn't waken.

It must be the fragrance of the chrysanthemums in my hands, it takes so little to bring childhood back to life. What I feel isn't grief. A November sadness, rather. Regret that those days have gone, reduced forever to a fine dust. Already I mix up periods, words, circumstances, places. Was that picture taken in the house on 9ᵉ Avenue or on 1ère? And who is that woman I saw a couple of times? She used to visit us, it seems to me. I will always be amazed that it never occurred to me to ask those things. But, I must admit, they didn't interest me. I used to run in my life as in a cage, never thinking that one day the wheel would come to a sudden stop. Now the wheel is motionless. I have all the time in the world to examine the past while it decomposes under my feet.

I never told my mother about the Capuchins' cemetery in Palermo. Catacombs dating back to the sixteenth century, where mummified bodies are suspended on the walls. Fascinated, I had quietly walked through all the sections. I had stood speechless before little Rosalia Lombardo, two years old, who died of pneumonia in the early twenties but was still perfectly preserved. She seemed to be asleep in her glass coffin, as serenely as my mother in the funeral home not so long ago.

That pagan custom has been abolished. Yet, in a way, it must have been comforting to visit one's dead, to take care of them, sew new clothes for them when the old ones grew too dusty. The living and the dead continued to live together. If I were a believer, I would think to myself, "Heaven is a place where we can go and spend Sunday afternoon with our departed." I would be less afraid of dying if I were sure my family could come and visit me. No sudden tearing away from life. A passage rather, a smooth transition.

Oddly enough, it didn't smell of death in the catacombs. Not of life either, its sweat, its breath, fresh or stale, its urine. It was like wandering through another world, a welcoming one, sensitive to mourning. There was nothing macabre about it. It was pleasant there, so pleasant I wanted to go back the next day. But I had to give up the silence and return to the racket of Palermo, a hellish din from motorbikes, honking horns, and cries hurled against the blackened stone. All those people were trying desperately to forget that their ancestors slept nearby.

We will eventually have to leave the cemetery. I wouldn't see my mother, I wouldn't buy her a new dress. I'll go away unconsoled, leaving her these flowers that will have wilted by tomorrow. If they don't freeze, that is. The florist put them into tiny water-filled tubes to preserve them, but what's the use? It doesn't ease my conscience. My mother should not have been buried here, in this arctic wind, even if it was her wish. But we live in a world where everything happens too quickly, where matters of death are settled like everyday transactions: coffin or urn, church service or civil ceremony, bouquets of roses or carnations? Consider the options, make decisions. You won't have time to think, you won't have time to let yourself go.

"You mustn't let yourself go." My mother's words again. Yet she cried during my grandfather's funeral service. I don't remember if she did for my father. I was too wrapped up in my own grief. Since my earliest childhood, I learnt to control myself. I am a sensible, level-headed woman. Reserved, reasonable, responsible, nice, and sociable. I can keep quiet, and I won't blow my top. There is no danger I'll behave like a woman I know who, while screaming, clung to her father's coffin when the time came to close it. They had to pull her away. What a difficult funeral. Honestly! But at least *she* had the courage to scream.

The wind is growing colder and colder, my mother more and more dead, her name more and more abstract. The leaves don't smell of anything anymore, nor do the chrysanthemums in my arms. I quickly put them down on the ground and flee, running all the way to my present life. The car starts at once, as usual. I play the music I listened to on the drive over. I prepare myself to see my familiar landscapes one more time. The old church where I used to go in the month of Mary, the college where I learnt Latin, the park where I walked so often with my mother, the park where I will never again walk with my mother, the park where I will never walk again.

I see the words *The End* appear before my eyes, and suddenly I feel like an actress in black and white who is about to leave her native land forever.

II
SNAPSHOTS

The Park

She walks, still very straight, along the Rivière Saint-François, and I follow close behind. Soon it will be summer, with the warm smell of foliage and glistening water. She stops, leans against the metal fence, screws up her eyes, and tries to catch sight of her heron. "In the evening it comes and lands on Lone Pine Rock," she whispers. She waits for him. I look for the duck and her ducklings, searching every ripple in the water. What if something happened to her? Here she is, swimming along while watching her little ones. Five, I count them with a smile. I can't remember how many there were last year. It's the same duck every year. I want to believe it. The same duck near the same park, the one from my childhood, the skating rink in winter, the swings in summer, the tall trees that have survived every ice storm, the grass that is almost too green, the four-leaf clover picked for good luck. And the river's rolling waters, less polluted now, they say, but is it really true? Here, the world is unchanging, my mother hasn't grown older. Neither have I, her daughter, or my brothers, or her grand-children.

The heron suddenly flies over the river, heading towards Lone Pine Rock, as my mother predicted. She points her crooked finger. She wants to make sure I really saw it. She laughs, it's a good omen.

The Market

She ambles down rue King in her floral dress. She has done her hair and put on the lipstick she only wears when she goes out. I am with her, while my brothers are at home with my grandmother. I'll help her carry the parcels. It's Friday, market day. We'll buy what we need for the week. First the meat, then the vegetables and the fruit. Finally, blue cheese from the fathers of Saint-Benoît. Always the same route, the same shopkeepers. My mother is joyful, she stops constantly, talks with old friends, neighbours, women she used to work with. She was born on rue Bowen, nearby, she knows a lot of people. "This is my daughter," she says whenever she introduces me. I get compliments, people think we look alike. My mother says I look like Louisa, the grandmother I never knew. And *I* want to look like my mother, who is so lovely in her flowered dress. When I'm grown up, I'll have a dress just like hers, and lipstick. I'll go to the market with my daughter. I'll have married a boy as handsome as the fruit-grower's son. During the holidays, he comes along with his father every Friday. The fruit grower and my mother chat together. "A charming man," she says. I lower my head, thinking about the son's blue eyes. I daydream about him, but I wouldn't want my mother to notice. I don't ask myself if my mother daydreams about the fruit grower. I don't puzzle over that yet.

The News

First she washes the glasses, then the plates, then the knives and forks. Finally, the pots and pans. That's the way to do it, the way my grandmother showed her, the way her neighbours do it. I watch them when I go to play with my girlfriends. I dry the dishes—I love that private time with my mother. Sometimes she confides in me. I already feel like a woman, I have grown a lot these past few months. But I don't know that I'll soon have my period, I don't know what a period is, or how children are made. My mother doesn't explain those kinds of things to me. She tells me about the neighbour who goes to church every evening while his wife looks after their five children. She tells me about women who never stop doing housework. She talks about her father's kindness, or her grandmother Émilie, who would surely have become president of a company, had she lived in our time.

Today, there is no serious talk. It's a holiday, Labour Day. It's mild out, and my brothers are playing on the lawn. My mother and I listen to the radio together at the sink. Suddenly the broadcast is interrupted. A solemn voice makes an announcement, and I see my mother's smile freeze. She puts down her dish towel, goes and presses her ear against the radio. Stunned, she blurts out, "The premier is dead. Maurice Duplessis is dead. That is big news for Quebec!" I don't understand what she means. She has never mentioned him to me. She never told me that my grandfather didn't like Maurice Duplessis.

Tea

She sits at the kitchen table, drinking her tea. My grandmother and I are with her. I am a big girl of six, I know how to behave myself. Usually my mother does housework, but not this morning. Last night she came home from the hospital. I am happy to see her, for I was afraid she wouldn't come back. She had a curettage, I know what that is. She lost the baby she was expecting, they had to clean her womb, that's a little pocket in the stomach for babies. My mother suddenly lifts her skirt a little and I see her thighs, they're pink, a reddish pink, and I feel dizzy, I am going to faint. It's only tincture of iodine, to disinfect, Mama explains, like what she puts on our knees when we fall.

I wonder if it hurt when they cleaned my mother's womb. I open my ears wide so I won't miss anything of what she tells my grandmother. She didn't carry that baby the same way as us, it would surely have been disabled—it's better to have lost it. And my grandfather had said after my little brother was born, "Three children is enough for you." He didn't like big families. My mother repeats those words so she'll feel better, but *I* don't feel better. I wanted another baby in the house, as when my brothers didn't walk yet. But I don't tell my mother.

Classical College

She is just back from my school, looking very chic in the spring coat she made herself. Sister Marie du Sacré-Coeur wanted to talk to her. She is my teacher in sixth grade, she came from France to teach us. She knows lots of things, and she is beautiful, cheerful, and patient. She doesn't scold us. We are fond of her, my girlfriends and I. She told my mother that I should go to classical college. I'll skip grade seven, but I'll catch up fast. And I won't be alone, one of my classmates is going too. "It's a dream come true," my mother murmurs. Next year, I'll begin my classical studies, I'll learn Latin and, later, Greek. She laughs, "Your grandfather would have been pleased."

Sister Marie du Sacré-Coeur has arranged everything. I'll go and take the entrance exam at the college, at the top of the hill, on avenue du Parc, and then we'll ask the government for assistance. Since last year, girls like me have been able to get an education. Under Duplessis, it was the parents who had to pay. That would have been impossible in our family. I see a furrow appearing between my mother's brows, but quite soon her smile returns. "You and your brothers were born at just the right time," she says. "Long live Jean Lesage! We, too, are entitled to have our children receive an education."

The House

She sits in the creaking rocking chair, the one in which she so often gave us the bottle, the one of the colic attacks and ear infections. Behind her, the dome of what used to be the Saint-Vincent hospital, where I was born. And, hidden by the trees, the house my grandfather had built. She has lived in this apartment for over twenty-five years, but her heart has stayed in "the house," as she calls it. She moved there at nine years of age and didn't leave until she was sixty-nine, except for short interludes. Four years in Toronto, two in an apartment in Sherbrooke, two in Drummondville, and one year in Victoriaville. Then we went back to the house. That's where my grandmother died, as well as my father.

She likes it here, in this building on rue Bowen, right near the park. She met up again with old girlfriends from primary school, and with a little neighbour she used to look after. She goes for a walk every day along the river. She also likes to take the bus to the Carrefour de l'Estrie. But it isn't *the house*. Sometimes, when I visit her, we lengthen our walk, making a detour through rue Kennedy North. We stop in front of the house. Her eyes take on a faraway look. Beautiful images stream by in her memory, mixed, I'm sure, with profound sorrows. I wait. I wait until words come back to her. Soon she sighs, "That's all finished now." She resolutely walks on, draws my attention to the setting sun, the fragrance of a blooming lilac, or the foliage of a maple tree. She leaves her old life behind, until our next walk.

Rue Kennedy

The 1ère Avenue Nord, that's where *the house* is, the one my grandfather had built. Until John F. Kennedy is shot in the head. Over and over we see him die on the television. It's all everyone talks about, at the college, at the garage where my father works, in town. The city council has decided that our street will soon be called rue Kennedy. My mother disagrees. He wasn't *our* president. "We aren't Americans." My mother doesn't like the United States. They want to control the planet. They'll do anything, threats, assassinations. She is proud of Fidel Castro, he pulled off his coup. He didn't let himself be pushed around at the Bay of Pigs. The Americans are always at war. My New England cousins had to go and fight. "Thank goodness we don't live there!" She is thinking of my brothers, "War is even more terrible when you have boys."

It's out of the question that the name of our street should be changed. Several neighbours share her opinion. My mother rises up in arms. I hear new words at home, *petitions, door-to-door*. People confer over the telephone or on the sidewalk. I see lists with many names go around, the City should be made to reconsider its decision. One day we learn that we no longer live on 1ère Avenue Nord. My mother has lost her battle. She turns the page. She says one should never look back.

The Lobby

She is sitting beside her friends in the residence's lobby. You'd think you were in a funeral home—impersonal armchairs, impersonal plants, impersonal décor—but no one seems to notice and I never make any comments, I keep quiet. The bus from Montreal has now arrived. She knows it, she is waiting for me. She hasn't spotted me yet behind the glass door, she is talking, she laughs. Suddenly she sees me, she brightens, gets up, comes over to open the door. I greet the row of women who are spending their afternoon killing time. I'm afraid I may become like them. Why worry, though? My mother keeps herself quite busy—reading, crossword puzzles, the television news, her walks. She isn't bored. At least, that's what she says.

I stop for a moment and make conversation. They are my mother's friends. She likes it when her daughter makes a good impression. And with the passing of time I have grown fond of these women, I have got to know them. "Everything is fine," one of them says, "God is good." We head towards the elevator. My mother smiles. She waits for the door to close. Then, frowning, she blurts out, "God may be good, but he's forgotten about a hell of a lot of people." I jump, I'm not accustomed to such crude language from her.

A Rest

She takes a brief rest, coming to sit with us on the wine red sofa, opposite the piano. My girlfriends adore my mother, they feel understood. They tell her about their loves at first sight, their heartbreaks, their plans. I feel a little jealous, and proud of her too. I have an exceptional mother, since my girlfriends love her. But I don't tell her anything, I don't want her advice. Today, no outpouring of secrets. We are in a state of shock. One of our classmates has left the college, she won't finish her year. During recess, girls whispered that she was going to get married. Get married at sixteen? She, especially, the best-behaved girl in our class? We didn't even know she had a sweetheart. *We* want to get married, but not right away. Later, when we've finished our education. My mother approves. Studying is important, a husband may die or leave, anything can happen nowadays. D. will go into social work, L. plans to study psychology, C. will teach music. I am going to teach too, but French. My mother smiles, she is pleased. When I performed in plays, I wanted to become an actress. I'm ashamed I had such a crazy idea. Those dreams aren't for people like us.

The Hospital

She sits in a very high bed that is all white. Yesterday evening, during supper, she cried out, then water ran down between her thighs and everyone stopped eating. My aunt told my uncle to go and take her to Hôtel-Dieu hospital right away. I stayed with my cousins, they took me to my grandfather and grandmother's house. This morning my cousins said to me, "You have a little brother." I don't know what a little brother is, but he's with my mother at the hospital, we are going to see him. They put me in a yellow dress with flounces, and curlers in my hair. They told me I was just as pretty as Shirley Temple. I don't know who Shirley Temple is.

    Mama has a funny smile on her face in her white bed. She likes me better with straight hair and bib overalls, I know. Too bad for Shirley Temple. But she doesn't tell my cousins, they're fond of curly hair, and they so much enjoy making dresses with flounces for me. I suck my thumb. I wish Mama would come home. She'll come home, she promises, with the little brother. Now I know what that is, it's a big doll that pees for real. Perhaps she'll let me play with it. It's even better than a cat.

The Residence

She holds out the letter she received to show me. The building where she has lived for over twenty years has been sold, and it will become a seniors' residence. She is up in arms about it, she'll have to take her meals in the dining room, and there will be a cleaning lady. "Cooking keeps me busy," she says. "What will I do with my days now? And I don't want to have a stranger poking her nose into my business." If she refuses, she'll be forced to move. Her parents lived on rue Bowen when she was born. She loves the park where she goes for her daily walk. She can gaze at the trees for as long as she wants, and at her river, and Lone Pine Rock, and her heron in summer. Several friends of hers live in the building. She wonders what decision they'll make. No doubt some will leave. "I'm not the only one who is furious." Beneath the anger, I sense anxiety, sadness, and helplessness. It's no joke for her to feel powerless against fate. Not for me either. I can't do anything to help her, only let her speak her mind.

Suddenly the telephone rings in the living room. She goes to answer it, becomes animated, and her smile returns. She puts the receiver down and looks at me. Residents are organizing a protest march around the building. I ask her if she is going. She answers firmly, "There is plenty of fight left in me."

The Garage

She asks us to get ready, we'll be leaving soon. We're going to see my father at the garage where he works. During the week, he is the janitor, and on weekends, night watchman. On Sunday after supper we walk up the hill of rue King as far as 11^e Avenue. We could make that trip with our eyes closed. My father is happy to see us. "It breaks the monotony for him," my mother says. A whole night is a long time!

We all sit down together in the showroom, among the new cars. They stir our imagination. We don't have a car. Later, if we study hard, we'll be able to buy one, and take holidays, and travel. We won't need to be careful about everything, like our parents. But they don't complain. My father likes his fellow workmen—he always comes home with good jokes. My mother laughs along with him. He used to be a guard at the prison, but he didn't like that. My mother is glad my father is working. When he was ill, she had trouble making ends meet. Now she can sleep peacefully. But I can tell that she's worried at seeing him spend the night all by himself in that building full of dark corners. There could be thieves. The other guard has a big dog. My father doesn't want one, he says he's not afraid. But I'm like my mother, I get a knot in my stomach every time I kiss my father goodbye.

The Album

She puts a Laura Secord chocolate box filled with photographs on the table, she wants to show me Émilie in her long black dress. It was the nun's dress her grandmother began to wear when she turned thirty. She laughs, "The age when women became old." I do the calculation. Émilie died at ninety-three, so she felt old for more than sixty years. I shudder. My mother doesn't comment. She has slipped back into her memories. Nicolet, the convent, her cousins, Grandfather Louis, the baker, people so familiar to me that I feel I have known them, too. She would have been a good novelist. She is an excellent storyteller.

Suddenly, as if she just had a flash of inspiration, she gets up, slowly making her way to her bedroom. She returns at once with three brand new albums. "I've decided to give each of you your childhood photographs. The time has come." My heart sinks, I know very well what she means. She holds an album out to me with a multi-coloured cover, in blended shades. Tints bright or dark, cheerful or serious, bold or discreet. Like my mother. She simply says, "This is for you."

Reading

My mother reads with a furrowed brow in her armchair. She finds that on the television it's always the same stories. And she is going deaf, but won't admit it. "People mumble nowadays, I can't understand them." She would rather read. She has time for it now. Since my father died, she has had to keep herself occupied. Whenever I come, I bring her books. She has read all of Gabrielle Roy, the memoirs of Simone de Beauvoir, the novels of Marguerite Duras, and Karen Blixen, and Nina Berberova. Also Anne Hébert, but she didn't like that. Too violent. She didn't like *The Sorrows of Young Werther* either, although she had asked me for it. "Killing yourself for love, that's a bit much." But she adored Don Quixote and his Dulcinea, and Sancho. And *Remembrance of Times Past*. She prefers the classics to the latest novels. "At my age," she says, "you want to read books that last, important books."

With reading, one is never bored. She gets that from her father. Before he was married, he went to work in Ottawa so he could read the books on the Index. You couldn't do that in Quebec. It's a disgrace, I think, but my mother doesn't get worked up about it, such was life in those days. She doesn't feel like getting angry anymore, she wants to look on the bright side now. She doesn't have much time left, why spoil what remains?

The Outing

She is standing in her bedroom, in front of the mirror above her chest of drawers. She tucks her hair into place, powders her cheeks, and takes out her lipstick. She examines herself, smiling at her image to buck herself up. Last night she hesitated a long time before picking a dress to wear. We talked it over, and listened to the weather forecast. She finally decided she'd wear the blue one. It's not too dressy, just right. She wants to look her best, we are going to see her doctor. He is the grandson of her old remnant shopkeeper. He reminds her of the years when she used to sew late into the night. She likes him, but is afraid of him. What if he finds something wrong with her, and decides to send her to the hospital or even a nursing home? I try to reassure her, I keep telling her, "Everything will be fine, you'll see." But she won't listen.

In a little while, the doctor will check her heart, take her pulse and blood pressure, ask her about her sleep, her appetite, her arthritis. She'll quickly say yes to everything so there will be no uncertainty in his mind about the state of her health. As usual, he'll end with, "You are going to live past a hundred." And she'll relax, beaming at him. She'll almost skip along, chatter brightly while waiting for the taxi, decide to order chicken when she gets home. And I, with a rush of emotion, will want to believe we'll have our mother for a long time yet.

The Event

She sits at the table, near the window. She is having a rest, drinking her tea. I sit across from her, and I tell her about the big event of the day. I can't get over it. One of our teachers has fallen head over heels in love with a woman. He has just left his wife and four children for her. In our class we are filled with admiration. Isn't it wonderful that a man his age can still follow his heart, and change his life? I would like to be just like him. Brave, determined. Adventurous.

At the end of the table, my mother lifts her cup to her lips, then slowly puts it down again on the tablecloth. She listens to me in silence, she frowns. When she frowns, it's a bad sign, she totally disagrees with me. But she listens, she lets me finish. Then she utters in one breath, "Have you thought about the poor woman who is left alone with four children?" Obviously, my mother doesn't understand a thing about passion or the spirit of *peace and love*. I get up, leaving the kitchen, my mother, and her outdated ideas. I won't tell her anything anymore.

The Meal

She sits upright in her chair in the dining room. She has invited me this evening, she wants to introduce the residents that share her table to me. She doesn't remember that I came a couple of weeks ago. She is losing her memory, and I'm trying to get used to it. There are five of us around the table, four women and one man. There are few men at the residence they die younger, it's a known fact. The food isn't bad, just insipid, ordinary, as in cafeterias. I ask everyone questions while I eat: how is your health, how are things going, how are the children. Answers come quickly. I bring a touch of joy to the meal. It isn't much, I know, but I can't do more.

Someday I'll be in a residence like this one. I watch these women of a previous era who worked day and night, bringing up large families. Monsieur R. was a nurse at the hospital nearby. My mother barely talks. She listens, but she is growing more and more deaf, so she doesn't really venture into conversation anymore. I slowly repeat to her what is being said. She agrees, and smiles. With a pang of sadness, I wonder if she eats in silence when I'm not here. Does she feel bad about it? But they look after her at the table, the residents are fond of her. "Your mother is so nice," they keep telling me. And I agree, she hasn't turned sour. She has no serious illness, I have to say. She is not in pain, she appreciates what she has. She has managed to age well.

Bedtime

She sits down in the bed, with us around her. We smell of perfumed soap, sheets dried in the sun, clean pajamas. It's Saturday, the evening when we're given our bath. She stoked up the wood stove to have hot water, and washed us in the bathtub one after the other. We'll be clean for Sunday Mass. At our house there are days for each activity. On Monday, it's the washing, on Tuesday the ironing, on Wednesday and Thursday the sewing, and, when it's necessary, some shopping. On Friday, after the grocery shopping, it's housework. On Saturday, we all have a bath. And on Sunday, after Mass, my mother only cooks. But every evening she reads us a story.

Tonight, she opens the book by Tante Lucille. She'll tell us the story of *The Strawberry Fairy of the Île d'Orléans*. The Île d'Orléans is a real island, near Quebec City. Our ancestress Éléonore lived there, my mother says. There are strawberries there, but no fairies. Fairies only exist in stories, like genies, and Santa Claus. But I don't tell my brothers, they're too small. I pretend to believe in the strawberry fairy. She is beautiful in the picture, she brings happiness. I like my mother's stories, as they always end well. Then my mother will tuck us in, give us a kiss on our forehead, and turn off the light. I will try to stay awake to hear what's being said in the kitchen.

The Flood

Her voice is clear on the telephone this morning, and cheerful. She proudly tells me about her exploits. Last night, the waters of the river began to rise and rise. The residents were ordered to evacuate the building. They would be taken to a school gymnasium. She hadn't wanted to call us, she went outside with her toothbrush and a few clothes. But downstairs, on the bus, she decided to go back to her apartment. She just couldn't bring herself to leave everything behind. Surely the water wouldn't reach the fifth floor. Several of her friends followed her. Like my mother, they spent the night in their apartments. "This isn't my first flood. Those so-called rescuers haven't seen anything yet." She often tells me about the floods of her youth. In one picture, she is in a rowboat that makes its way down the middle of rue Saint-François. She sounds as if she is having fun. "Why are people afraid of everything nowadays?"

Next time, it would be wiser to leave the building, I gently try to tell her, there are risks. "Risks?" She starts to laugh. She slept in her bed, and slept well, in fact. Next time, she'll do the same thing. She won't start now obeying men younger than her grandsons. Or me or my brothers. Let's be very clear about that.

The Telephone

She wakes up, in her white bed, as fresh as if she were at a hotel. Then she catches sight of me speaking on the telephone. She asks who I'm talking to. I tell her, "To J.-P., your son-in-law. He'll be here tomorrow." Her face lights up, she wants to say a few words to him. She really is in full possession of her faculties, you'd almost think the doctor lied to me a few minutes ago. She is speaking in a firm, joyful voice, and says, "I'm expecting you, J.-P. I look forward to seeing you." Then she hands the phone back to me. I feel as though I were dreaming. Here is the nurse, she is coming to make sure everything is all right. My mother asks her who she is, then tells us both to go to bed, she wants to sleep. The nurse smiles at me and leaves. For now, there is no need for drugs, my mother isn't in any pain. Is it a miracle? I tell her I'll sleep here, in the armchair. She checks if this is true. I sit down and close my eyes. She soon goes back to sleep.

Half past eight, a pitch black night, an icy night, a merciless night. In the darkened room, I am wondering if my mother will still be alive tomorrow morning. I wait, I sit up, I prepare myself, the coming hours could be difficult. I say *difficult* to avoid the word *unbearable*. I wish my mother would die right away, since we can't do anything more for her. I don't want to see her suffer. If I were a believer, I would implore God, the Blessed Virgin, and all the saints. I know there is nothing I can do. Except press the bell to ask for morphine.

Cards

She knits her eyebrows. They are black, still thick in spite of her ninety-six years. She sorts the cards, holds them out to me. She says, "Make a wish." The wish of the four aces. I know all about it, my grandmother showed me how to tell fortunes with cards as soon as I was old enough. I shuffle, eyes heavenward, as if I believed in it. And my mother smiles at me, as if *she* believed in it. Here we go. She spreads the cards out on the table, and I watch her. We would both like the four aces to turn up side by side. I have made a real wish, one never knows! But the four aces are separated by the seven of spades. "A slight disappointment," my mother says. She seems as let-down as I am, and asks me if I want to start over. I shake my head, perhaps tomorrow. I may not believe in these superstitions, but I don't wish to be disappointed a second time.

Now it's my turn to tell her fortune. I ask her to shuffle. My heart beats faster, I would like there to be no spades. Only red cards, love, surprises, presents, money. I observe her while she shuffles, her eyes heavenward too. We both smile. Then she hands me the pack and I spread the cards out on the table. She watches closely, still frowning. Suddenly she raises her crooked finger, showing me death, beside the queen of clubs. And I say, too quickly, "That's T., J.-P.'s aunt, the doctor gives her only a few months." She relaxes, agrees. Yes, T., why didn't she think of it? Death is not for her, death will not come.

The Appointment

She helps me to put on my coat and my beret. I'm going home with her, I'm happy. My mother has come to school. She had asked for an appointment with my teacher after classes. My grandmother is looking after my little brothers. She wanted Mme G. to let me write with my left hand. My girlfriends are right-handed, and their homework looks beautiful. When *I* write with my right hand, the letters are all crooked. I feel ashamed, I'd rather stay home. She said, "Your grandfather was left-handed too, it's not an illness." I know, we still have his tailor's scissors, special scissors just for him. He has always earned his living.

My mother explained to Mme G. that I've never been able to eat with my right hand, or to draw, or cut anything out, or throw a ball. I was born like that. There are many of us. It seems there would be thousands of left-handed people if no one interfered with them. Mme G. listened, then said it was all right because it's what my mother wanted. Now I'll be able to write in my own way. I'll have clean homework too, and pink angels in my exercise books.

The Lottery

She has put on her dressing gown, she rocks herself in front of the television set, her lottery tickets in her hand. She is waiting for the results of Lotto 6/49. She says with a laugh, "Five million dollars! I would be satisfied with a hundred thousand." What would she do with money at her age? Get new clothes? Travel? "I don't go out anymore, I am happy at home." She isn't lying. But on lottery nights, she fantasizes. She would share the money with us, her children, but she'd worry a little. What if her grandchildren didn't want to work anymore? The devil finds work for idle hands, as we all know. Everyone in the family has toiled away, she more than anyone, like her parents. And during the Great Depression, my father carried sacks of coal up to the third floor for a dollar a day.

Finally, Loto-Québec's drawing machine appears, along with the hostess, all smiles. The numbers come out one by one. She strains to hear. She circles a first number on her ticket, then a second one, but no third. The machine stops. She sighs with disappointment, "I never win." All that money thrown out of the window over the years! Every week, she decides to stop betting. But I persuade her, why deny herself this little bit of fun? She starts laughing again, she concludes, "It's a voluntary tax, in fact. It's good for Quebec."

The Catalogue

Smiling with delight, my mother brings me the new Eaton's catalogue, the one for spring. The postman just delivered it. Tonight, while having her tea, she will leaf through it, then jot down ideas for clothes she is going to make for us. Dresses for her and for me, outfits for my brothers, pants for my father. And I, I'll spend hours gazing at each page. I find the women beautiful, well-dressed, with nice-looking hair. The tables are always perfect, not a stain on the tablecloth, not a plate that doesn't match. And the sofas are fashionable. Later, I'll have a house like these, too. And a husband as elegant as a model. And children who are clean, even after they've played outside all day.

My mother no longer dreams. She makes do with the life she has: spilled glasses of milk, an apron with sauce spots, the old plates and dishes, our pants stained with grass and mud in the evening. She doesn't scold us, she often repeats something my grandfather used to say, "You can't hang children up on the wall." Even so, *I* have ambition, I am going to try to do better than her. It's all so beautiful in the Eaton's catalogue, just like on television, in *Father Knows Best*.

Heaven

She lies on white silk, with white bouquets surrounding her. You'd almost think she was asleep, as in her hospital bed the night she died. We, her children and grandchildren, crowd around her. We look like abandoned puppies, even though we aren't that age anymore. "Grandma looks like a statue," my grandson says. I pull myself together and try to explain, but the child doesn't understand. No one understands death in fact, but I tell him a story about paradise where people rest forever. One day, when we, too, are very old, our souls will go to heaven, high up in the sky, higher than the clouds, and we'll go and be with Grandma. Puzzled, the little boy looks at me, he doesn't want to go to heaven, he wants his great-grandmother to come back to her apartment, surrounded by living flowers she lets him water in the summer on the balcony.

The little boy will grow up, he'll have children perhaps, and he will look at me lying on white silk too, surrounded by white flowers. Then *he* will explain to his grandson or granddaughter that Grandma now lives with the angels. And that in the future we will all be together again, just like on New Year's Day.

The Blouse

She shows me the pattern of the top she has just cut out for herself. A blue grey blouse with three-quarter sleeves. In summer, she no longer wears anything low-cut or sleeveless. "Old people are like birds," she says. "They are more attractive with their plumage." I tell her she is still beautiful, with a rosy complexion, and fewer wrinkles than much younger women. She looks at me, but I only half convince her, she doesn't like her body anymore. Growing old is a bereavement. I experience it too. I remember the first line at the corner of my eye, the first puffiness below my eyelid.

She has fallen silent and I don't go on about it. What's important has been said. I still find her beautiful, she heard me, my words will sink in, I hope. My mother is old, I won't be able to console her. We face old age alone, we make the great leap into the abyss alone one day. That is the tragedy of our condition. My mother doesn't rebel. I don't either. What's the use?

Suddenly, she regains her energy. She gets up, gathers the fabric and the pattern from the table, takes a few steps towards her bedroom. Then she stops, turns towards me and throws me a look. "Now is the time to show your arms," she fires off with a laugh. "Don't wait!"

Twelfth Night

She got up very early this morning, put the turkey in the oven, cooked the cranberries. Yesterday she prepared the tourtières, and made her cake. My grandmother made the *sucre à la crème*. The refrigerator is full to bursting. Soon my father's whole family will be here. On New Year's Day we go to my uncle's place, and on Twelfth Night the family comes here. But the real feast is Labour Day, when another uncle invites us over to Saint-Antoine-sur-Richelieu. He bought the family farm, has a big dog, cows, chickens and a colony of cats in the barn. I like the big house, with the verandah all around it. My aunt lets my brothers and me run about. And in the attic there are cannonballs from the days of the Patriotes. They fought against the English, my mother said. My uncle always pronounces the word *Patriotes* in a quivering voice. He is proud of them, proud of his family, who hid them. And so am I, because it's my family.

Tonight, my uncle from Saint-Antoine will come too, with my aunt. They've left the farm with my cousin, since there's less work in the winter than in the summer. I can hardly wait, my uncle has so many things to tell us about. *He* remembers his mother. He'll get angry when he talks about the orphanage, the nuns were harsh, he hates them. My father will smoke his cigarettes without uttering a word. My mother won't say anything either, it's not her family, she prefers to keep quiet. I know what she'll say tomorrow. "With four or five hundred children, the nuns did what they could." My father will agree with her, there were some he was fond of. But *he* doesn't remember his mother. He was too small when she died.

Blackmail

She paces up and down the living room, her face haggard. My aunt hasn't called her in five days. I try to reassure her, her sister is giving her the cold shoulder, that's all. Sometimes she decides not to keep in touch. My mother holds out for a while, but always calls her in the end, to ask her over for dinner. "She is blackmailing you," I say, "this time, you should ignore her." But I'm wasting my breath. Her anxiety will grow and grow. She will imagine the worst, a fall, a heart attack, her sister lying helpless in her apartment. She will give in, as usual. She will lift the receiver, and dial my aunt's number. I feel tiny needles digging into my neck, one by one, down to my jaw.

I wish my mother had resisted for once. There's no point showing my anger, I would only be adding grief to anxiety. She'll say, "Your aunt is ill." I've been hearing this since I was old enough to talk, but I won't accept that my mother is the one who pays. She is entitled to a peaceful old age. I know only too well that she feels responsible for her. Even worse, guilty, like the survivors of an accident when the family has died. I blame my aunt. She behaves like a tyrannical child. I blame my mother for her indulgence. This evening, in the dimly lit living room, I'll hear, "You can't understand." And I don't want to understand. I've never wanted to understand why my mother persists in loving her sister who shows no gratitude towards her, while we, her children, do everything possible not to give her cause for worry.

The Mending

She stands before me, in the old nightgown she refuses to throw out, her hair dishevelled. I am out of luck, I thought she would wake up later. She asks hoarsely, "What are you doing?" She sees that I am repairing the hem of one of her skirts. I answer calmly, "The hem of your skirt is undone." It is my turn now to look after her clothes. To make sure they are clean, ironed, mended. A moment ago, I slipped a dress that is beyond repair into my suitcase, as she refused to throw it out. Fortunately, with her memory getting shakier all the time, she'll forget about her dress, about her skirt, and about the slight disagreement we had last night. "I don't want you to do my laundry anymore. I can still do it." We argue more and more often when I come, I can't get used to it.

I am preparing myself for another disagreement this morning. I clam up. I continue with my work, my left hand moving back and forth, the needle, the woollen garment—just like she showed me when I was a teenager. She actually takes a breath, a nasty furrow etches itself at the corners of her mouth, she points her finger at me. Then she utters slowly, "Writing is your business, I keep out of it. But sewing is my business. I don't want you to touch my clothes. Do you hear me?"

The Birth

She doesn't have her usual voice, I sense it as soon as I pick up the phone. She is elated. She is now a grandma for the fourth time, another girl. Two boys and two girls, she feels she has all she could wish for. There would have been four of us too, if she hadn't had a miscarriage. I don't know if she thinks about that tonight, I don't mention it. She has always loved children. It was bliss when we were little, she often says. In her eyes, images of us drift by, our white boots, our toys, our laughter, our tears, and the illnesses brought home from school, the nights spent nursing us. She is sorry to see us grown up. Life goes by too quickly but, fortunately, she has grandchildren! And she cradled this rosy little girl all day long. How comforting it is, a baby in your arms!

Since my father died, it has become even more precious, a small body that presses itself against her skin, that moist warmth, that smell of tepid milk and powder. They are the only caresses she has left. And our kisses, at each of our visits. Big kisses on the cheeks, given too quickly, too discreet. I should learn to hug my mother, but I don't know if I'd be able to, I don't know how she would react. I got my reserve from her. The two of us are caught in the same net.

Breakfast

She plods along, leaning on her walker. Smiling, she finally arrives at the table, greeting J.-P. and me. I pull her chair back, and help her to sit down. I bring her an orange and a cup of coffee. She lets her eyes wander around her, then looks at us in surprise. She asks us where her mother and sister are. I instinctively withhold the truth. I lower my eyes and mumble that they have gone out. "Already?" she asks, looking at the clock. She doesn't add anything, takes a sip of coffee. I head for the toaster with a sense of relief. Perhaps it would be better to tell her the truth. Am I being kind, or cowardly? Every morning, she looks for her dead, her mother and her sister, often my father. But, oddly enough, never my grandfather, as if she had stopped waiting for him a long time ago.

I listen in from the kitchenette. She answers J.-P., who is making conversation with her. She had a good night, she marvels at the sun, you'd never know it's the middle of December. Then suddenly her voice drops. She murmurs, "What's the name of the woman who is with you this morning?" I hear, "Your daughter. Your daughter." And she, right away, "I did think I'd seen her before." I have a funny look on my face when I return with the toast and the jar of jam. It is the first time my mother doesn't recognize me.

The Carrefour

She glances at her watch while she skips breezily along. We'll be on time—we'll be able to catch the next bus to the Carrefour de l'Estrie. We'll go to Eaton's and stroll around the ladies' department, then we'll go and see the clothes that are on sale. Often we find a sweater there, or a blouse or a coat at a ridiculously low price. No one will know we paid so little. My mother will feel she has outwitted the whole world. Next, we'll have a bite to eat and do the rounds of the ladies' wear shops all through the mall. There are at least fifty of them. Clothes bind us together, it's the memory of my tailor grandfather. And of my grandmother, who loved hats. As if the years hadn't passed.

She doesn't like stores where the saleswomen breathe down our necks. She only wants to look, to know how long the skirts are, and what colours are in fashion. She scrutinizes cuts and fabrics. "Today, with synthetic fabrics," she says every time, "clothes look cheap." She lifts up a tag, grimaces when she reads the price. "Honestly, women are being robbed." I don't remind her that women have jobs nowadays; they don't have time to sew anymore. I let her dream about her earlier life. Sewing ideas suddenly come to her, her voice sounds young again, she'll open her Singer machine the very moment fall arrives, she promises herself she will. And I promise myself to go shopping with her more often.

The Conversation

She talks in a hushed voice to my grandmother in the kitchen. She thinks I'm asleep. But I prick up my ears to hear. Tomorrow, she'll go and buy things for my aunt at Saint-Michel-Archange. It's been ages since I last saw her. My grandfather took her to Quebec City in an ambulance. "That's what killed him," my grandmother says. He was very upset, he became ill right after, a stomach ulcer. I know the whole story. My aunt did odd things. The doctors weren't able to cure her, not even those my grandparents paid in Montreal. She couldn't be kept at home anymore. "Mental illness isn't like the flu," Mama sighs.

My grandmother feels very sad, but she is stronger than my grandfather apparently. She says every day that we must keep our spirits up. She means that we mustn't let ourselves go. My mother doesn't let herself go either. She doesn't have time with all the housework. And my grandmother asks her to send lots of things to my aunt. Clothes, jam, chocolates. "We had to place her in an institution," my grandmother says, "but we're thinking of her." Mama adds, "Yes, we're thinking of her."

The Movies

She is too old for that now, she says firmly. When she was a child, she went to the movies every week with her father and little sister, but now she prefers to stay home. I insist without much conviction, but I know she won't change her mind. This refusal to leave her apartment is almost pathological. As if her world would collapse while she was out. *I will continue travelling, seeing shows and movies until the end.*

She slips into her old cotton dressing gown and settles herself in the rocking chair, all smiles. She says, "We're going to chat." That's what she wants, to talk, she doesn't have anyone to chat with anymore now that she lives alone. I prepare myself to listen to stories from the past she has told me a hundred times. Her eyes light up, she is back in 1927, in the Ford her father has bought. They are taking their Sunday drive, and they have a flat tire. Everyone has to get out so my grandfather can repair it, "We had fun," she says. And now here is grandmother Émilie, who used to tell her daughters, "Turn off the radio, the neighbours are going to think we're having an argument." She wonders what her grandmother would say about life today: television, the internet, Skype, and the phone calls she can make to Hong Kong to talk to her grandson. That was unthinkable in those days. She laughs heartily, seeming thirty years younger. After the television news, she'll say, "You see? We didn't need to go out. We had a lovely evening."

The Visit

Grandpa and Grandma are coming for a visit. I can't keep still, I jump up and down, I run about, I shout. I want them to stay with us for a long, long time. Since we moved to Drummondville, I hardly ever see my grandfather, I miss him. Mama dresses us in our Sunday clothes to go to the station, it's a big day. Here they are at last, the two of them, they're walking towards us with their suitcase, smiling. Grandpa carries his good suit over his arm. Mama is surprised, no outings have been planned. She purses her lips but doesn't say anything. *I* don't care two hoots about that, Grandpa can wear whatever he likes as long as he plays with us. He is happy to see my brothers and me. He takes us for a walk every day, we must make the most of the summer. Now the smallest one is in the stroller. My older brother and I are big enough to walk.

One afternoon, he suddenly decides to turn back. He is very pale. My heart pounds in my chest. We quickly return home. The three of us will play together, quietly. My grandmother and mother have a strange look and they speak in hushed voices. But I have sharp ears, I manage to catch, "He doesn't have much longer to live." I know those words. They said them the other night too, when they thought we were asleep.

Sunday

My mother is radiant today. Her sister has agreed to come to the house even though I am there. Normally, she doesn't want to see me. We are having a glass of Cinzano. The three of us are talking like old friends who have met again after a long trip. I observe my aunt. She is a good conversationalist, has a keen memory, excellent taste, and a sense of humour. This woman has been beautiful, you can see it, you can understand that she has broken hearts. "More than I have," my mother will occasionally say. I wonder if there was jealousy between the two sisters. If so, there no longer is, Lucienne is a broken woman.

In my armchair, I face the indecipherable enigma my aunt represents for me. The enigma and the grief. She was born at a time when there were few resources. She paid dearly for it. As did my grandparents and my mother. It would be enough to make you cry. And yet the three of us are laughing. It's a wonderful day. We receive it like a gift.

The Portfolio

She opens the pale grey portfolio she keeps safely in the bottom drawer of her desk. Together, we are going to look at the reproductions of great paintings she collected before she got married. No housework or sewing on Sunday. We can take all the time in the world to examine each painting in detail. There is one I like better than the others, a little girl with the dress of a princess, but her face is sad, as if she were bored to death. I'm surprised every time, all little girls dream of being a princess. "A famous painting," my mother says. *Las Meninas* by Velasquez. I also like the reproduction Mama had framed that hangs above the piano, ballerinas in white tutus, on their toes, like the ones you see on Radio-Canada. It's by Edgar Degas, he painted many dancers. On Sundays, I learn names we never hear in school: Renoir, Monet, Delacroix, Goya, Michelangelo. But there are also names I don't want to remember. Like that of the painter showing a hare killed by a man with a feathered hat who stands beside his horse. I think he is cruel. I hate hunting, my father does too. We mustn't hurt animals, my mother often reminds us. But all the same we should get used to looking at works that don't appeal to us.

Nostalgia

She stands at the foot of my bed, terribly alive, like the mother she had been when I was thirty. Perhaps she did not die, almost a year ago, at the hospital. Perhaps I only imagined her death throes on that icy December night, and the morphine, and her calmed face, asleep for all time in white sheets. In the aura of slumber, I no longer remember her last autumn, lingering like winter. Then, bit by bit, it all comes back to me, her hospitalization in November, the visits to the doctor's office, the social worker, the search for an assisted-living residence. And the feeling that I was continually lying to her, the guilt, and the ever-present worry. I let these images drift by, they end up making their way slowly into my head. I can get up then, have my first cup of coffee, and start writing again: this story about her, my mother forever, my immortal mother.

Sometimes, on waking, I feel overwhelmed with nostalgia again, as though it had waited for my being asleep to revive. Struggling against it would be useless, the longing is stronger than me. I outwit it, end up trapping it, lull it to sleep for a while. I wonder how much time has to pass before we accept a mother's death. Could it be that we never completely accept it?

III

THE GRACE OF THE DAY

My mother constantly appears to me. It only takes the smallest thing: her old sewing machine in need of dusting, a word she used to say, or an ageless woman inching her way along the sidewalk. The smallest thing, really, and she is there. I would be able to talk to her, touch her, take her in my arms. But soon, like a slap, reality. The void, the vertigo of the abyss, the horror of nothingness. How could my mother die? How is death possible? Neither philosophy nor biology can ease my mind.

Why buy so many useless things, clothes, knickknacks, books we don't read, CD's we only play once? Why receive presents, and accumulate trinkets our children will throw away in just a couple of decades? I get absurd ideas—to ask my friends not to give me anything for Christmas or my birthday anymore. They could make donations instead to charity organizations, like Centraide or the SPCA. In stores, I now hesitate before picking up the slightest piece of clothing. I picture it in a large garbage bag by the side of the road. I can't understand why people are happy about the economic recovery. We will consume more, we are told. Unemployment will drop. But we'll continue using resources. The great wheel of capital will turn even faster, and we will load ourselves down even more. Human beings have never been able to learn from death.

I have embarked on a thorough decluttering of the house. I file, put away, and sort. I fill bag after bag so as not to impose that job on my daughter one day. I say with a laugh that I've reached the age of subtraction. That souvenir from my holiday in Italy, letters from a forgotten love, that theatre program, are they still important? And those photos—there are at least ten boxes of them—I'm sure I'll never have time to look at them. I put my camera away, actually. I don't want to collect photographs anymore, I don't want to have to get rid of them one day.

"We can't live our life preparing for death all the time," a friend told me. I lost my temper, and raised my voice. I am not preparing for death, I am slowly getting used to it, without sadness. I now live with a deep awareness that I too will lie down in the ground someday for all eternity. We cannot pretend we will escape it. You are dust, and to dust you shall return. Death is as real as the blue of the sky or the green of the trees. Losing someone we love marks us at the very core of our being. The grief fades in the end, but not the horror of death, which can resurface at the slightest pretext. Even if mourning leads to calm remembrance, it always leaves a melancholy halo.

I defended myself as if I were being sued. I should get used to it, though. Grieving people are not at all well thought-of, except in books or movies, where it's all right to take anything to extremes. Don't we need fortitude to live with the thought of death without sinking into gloom? The bereaved is a tightrope walker stepping forward on the wire while trying not to fall. It is not a question of denial, only of finding a balance between oblivion and stifling recollection, a line of sight that lets us enter the movement of reminiscence. If we look too closely at the abyss, we may lose our footing. And if we gaze into the distance, we don't see anything.

Since my visit to the cemetery, I have tried to imprint on my mind a thousand scenes involving my mother, so I may bring back to life forever this woman who was cheerful, irreverent, affectionate, self-righteous, stubborn, obstinate, argumentative, and sometimes sad in the dimly lit living room. If these numerous portraits of her were obliterated one day, how could I still have an image of myself? But I write. I write to anchor myself in reality. I agree with J.-B. Pontalis when he says that "writing is also a way to remain an imaginary child beside an absent mother." Our image of ourselves is rooted in our childhood.

I am creating a memory for myself, fighting against my own disappearance. I end up with a past that was happy, sometimes unhappy, with little brothers, an invented girlfriend, real girlfriends at school, cats, a guardian angel that slept with me at night, and scruffy dolls I put to bed in a wooden cradle. I now have a history again. I escape the fate of Eve, the only woman on earth who didn't have to mourn for her mother.

★★★

Let yourself be touched by the grace of the day. This phrase kept going around in my head even before I opened my eyes this morning. I lay very still for a few minutes, wondering what it tried to tell me. Everything's fine, have faith, yes, you don't need to be afraid, the day promises to be a gift, don't be afraid. You *are* afraid. But is it really fear? "We shouldn't let ourselves go," my mother and grandmother used to say. What were they afraid of? That the structure they had erected stone by stone within themselves might crumble?

The spectre of madness is never far away when a woman says she is afraid. "I am not mad. Do you think I am mad? Perhaps I am going mad," or, bluntly, "I am mad." Those confessions can be heard in private conversations between female friends. Deep inside every woman lives a feeling of uncertainty, a suspicion regarding her mental health. My mother and grandmother must have been no different. But they closed the slightest breach as they went along, they didn't want to be unable to cope. Still, when you write, you need to accept that things might get out of hand. This is what last night's sleep was telling me. Don't be afraid of foundering. Writing will protect you. Be willing to travel back even further into your childhood. You will be fine.

In this old photo in my album, I must be six months old. Mama carries me in her arms. She smiles blissfully, fascinated by her creation of flesh and blood, that chubby-cheeked baby holding out her hand to the camera. I always sensed that she had passionately wanted my brothers and me. As for my father, I never felt that having children was an accomplishment for him, or even something he desired. Did my mother and father talk about births? Did they plan them? I quizzed my mother about it one evening. Children, she answered, are the result of the *yes* pronounced during the marriage ceremony. Couples didn't discuss them. I'm sure that for many men fatherhood turned out to be the necessary evil that entitled them to love and sexuality.

And yet. In one photo, I am in my father's muscular arms. In another one, he watches me as I start to walk. In a third, he poses in a snowy landscape next to us, all of us wrapped up in cozy outfits sewn on the Singer machine. He never dresses us, doesn't feed us, doesn't give us our Saturday bath, but sometimes, before supper, he tells us stories. We have a father, a father who looks after his children in the way of the men of his time. It would seem that he learnt to love us. If he had been able to express himself, I am sure he could have said to us what Pierre Leduc wrote to his daughter in Bernard Émond's film *Tout ce que tu possèdes*: "I didn't want you to be born, but now a world you wouldn't live in seems impossible to me."

Once in a while my father may have pictured his life without his children. But he would never have admitted it. Those are things one doesn't say. My lingering image of him is of an inattentive man, who got annoyed now and then by the shouts and laughter of children ringing through the house. I don't remember him on the floor with us, pushing a tractor or a truck. Or in front of the Meccano set my younger brother got for Christmas, or cutting out pictures with us from the Eaton's catalogue. We were separated by an invisible screen, a glass wall.

Fortunately, there was my mother, who could act the part of the one "who walked through walls." She played with us, took care of us, talked to us. Later, she would help us with our homework and our lessons, and go pick up our report cards at school. She was proud to have children who were doing well. In fact, it's what she expected from us. Children who would have good jobs later on. And what did my father expect from us? Can an orphan who started working on a farm at eleven years of age want a privileged life for his children? He probably couldn't even imagine it. I would understand that later—too late—when my uncles, flabbergasted, said to him, "So your children have done well!" As if he weren't our father. I don't know what wound such words leave in the heart.

But my uncles were telling the truth. It was my mother who wanted us to get an education. I got one. And with it, I turned my back on my father's working-class environment, on his outdated language, his Norman pronunciation. He wasn't like the fathers of the other girls at the college, who spoke well, wore white shirts, and showed spotlessly clean nails. Professionals who didn't fear being out of work, didn't roll their cigarettes, and who owned a car and took their family to the seaside in the summer. "If we want our daughters to have a comfortable life, we need to give them an education," my mother once said to a woman who lived next door. I would meet a boy at university who would be sure to provide for me. And if I were unfortunate enough to be left a widow one day, I would be able to earn a living.

"The more you learn, the more you earn." *Qui s'instruit,*

s'enrichit. We all remember that slogan! The Quiet Revolution created an irreversible divide between us young people who began to go to college and our uneducated parents. It led to contempt for the working class, a latent, hidden, subconscious contempt encouraged by our teachers, who were preparing us to become society's elite. This involved leaving behind our families, their customs, and their values. Actually, parents no longer understood their children. The loss of our faith, contraception, free love, *beat* music—we talked as little as possible about it at home. In fact, we didn't talk about it at all in their presence. How do you feel when your children turn into strangers?

The only word that comes to me is *grief*. Those parents must have experienced intense grief. No doubt also a feeling of being duped, even rejected. My father never mentioned it. He didn't know how to express his emotions. My mother did discuss it with me. Sunday Mass was part of our culture. If we abandoned Catholicism, we would also abandon our French someday, and we would all end up speaking English. It was impossible to make her separate religion from language. She had kept the values of the resistance to assimilation. But she was sentimental as well: Latin, incense, statues, priestly ornaments, they were all part of a heritage passed on to her in her childhood.

One Sunday morning, I didn't go to Mass. My mother had lost the battle. She never talked about it again. After we left home, she stopped going to church. We were grown-up, so she didn't need to set an example anymore. Besides, like her father, she was not a believer, she admitted to me. My jaw dropped. All those nights of discussions about religious practice with us while she didn't believe? Obviously she was a woman of paradoxes.

For a child, ambiguous talk is always difficult. Enough time has to pass for us to understand, to read beneath the words, to go back several generations. My mother was not just part of her father's family, she also belonged to her mother's people, a family of practising Catholics that included nuns, devout aunts, priests, all of them accustomed to the Lent fast, the evening rosary, novenas, and retreats. She was proud of that. It was quite something to have had an aunt who was Superior General of the Soeurs grises, and a cousin who was a bishop. He had even confirmed me. Who else in my class could boast about that?

My mother must have been afraid I might reject a part of what she had taught me. Isn't that what she showed without knowing it by defending religious customs? She could tell very quickly that, in spite of my brand new atheism, my behaviour towards her hadn't changed. She stopped feeling threatened. She could stop being a practising Catholic. As for my father, he realized I had grown away from him as soon as I went to classical college. I am aware of that now. I am able to understand his grief.

★★★

What is mourning? What is mourning for a mother? And what is mourning for a mother by a daughter, an adult daughter, who no longer needs to have her diaper changed, or to be fed, washed, have her nose blown, her clothes mended, be given advice to, or scolded? Sorrow and relief, feelings of abandonment and freedom mixed together, an irreparable severing from her deepest roots, but, also, freedom. Freedom? Really? Even dead, a mother remains very much alive, with her voice, stooped figure, facial expressions, gestures, and her most ordinary comments. "Put on your hat, you'll catch cold. Don't forget your vitamins. You should eat broccoli."

Afterwards, we think we'll be able to write about everything concerning our mother. But, as it turns out, I still try to protect her memory. She changed my diapers, fed me, washed me, blew my nose, mended my clothes, gave me advice, scolded me, went to pick up my report cards at school, helped me with my homework, asked me my catechism questions every evening, and sewed so many dresses and coats for me late into the night. She will only die along with me on my own deathbed.

My mother has become more present than when she was alive. She practically takes up all the space. Flashes, images popping up out of the blue, spells of sadness, pangs of guilt. Mourning is a perfect breeding ground for guilt, which grows like a plant in the tropics, feeding on the slightest memory. An apple-tart recipe, a letter we rediscover, a woman bearing a vague resemblance to her, an incident we recall. And we say, "My mother was a good mother, in spite of what I may have held against her." I could have done more, gone to see her more often. Sherbrooke isn't so far, was I all that busy? Guilt, regret at having missed precious moments.

Guilt, that feeling that we didn't understand, that we were unfair towards her. Don't we often idealize our relationship with the departed? One sees women crying their eyes out over husbands they found insufferable a few years earlier. They have forgotten everything. And now I am just like them—it must be a normal stage. I have to make an effort to remember the final months. My mother growing weaker, more and more deaf, having difficulty walking. Her crumbling memory, the same ten anecdotes I heard over and over, my impatience, which I tried to keep under a bell jar. Yet I know she did what she could.

All the same, I was annoyed, angry that my mother who had been immortal up to then could no longer repel the attacks of death. She had no right to waste away, no right to let herself go. What did that anger hide? The prospect of abandonment, the feeling that a day would come when death would be too powerful for me? That, if I had no example, I would let go, too? Faced with our mother's death, we become a child again. We ask for the impossible. We demand what we cannot receive. Perhaps women are even more unfair towards their mothers than men.

Speaking about her mother, Simone de Beauvoir stated, "I would make her talk, I listened, I made comments. But because she was my mother, her displeasing sentences displeased me more than if they had come from another mouth." *I* could have written that. We never completely get over the loss of the good fairy of our childhood. Just as our mother never gets over the loss of the perfect little girl of her dreams. Mothers project themselves onto their daughters and the daughters onto their mothers. On either side arise impossibly high hopes and, naturally, disappointments.

I disappointed my mother several times. I left home as soon as I turned twenty, I took a two-year break from my undergraduate studies, I started smoking very early, I sometimes showed up in old jeans in front of her women friends just to annoy her. And that's not all. I have never felt guilty about those decisions. They are part of a child's detachment from its parents. My mother never blamed me for them. "Children should move away," she used to say. Even though it wasn't what she wished, she allowed us to move away. That is a priceless gift.

What I do reproach myself for is my inconsiderate behaviour. I would forget to call her on Sunday after I left Sherbrooke. I often let several weeks go by before going to see her. I didn't take enough interest in what interested *her*. I didn't support her enough after my father died. I wasn't a grateful-enough daughter for what she had done for me. I didn't understand my mother as I should have. I didn't love her as I should have. How many of us blame ourselves after our parents' death?

I had the good fortune of having a mother who, without being perfect, gave me enough to be able to manage in life. Did I show her enough love? Was I a good-enough daughter? What sort of love is expected from a child? Can you put yourself before your mother? My mother would have said yes. My grandmother too. Neither one tried to instill guilt in my brothers or me. That should be sufficient to soothe my conscience, but it isn't.

Perhaps guilt fuels our grief. Every day, it rekindles the flame of our love for those we cherish, it stirs our memory of them, ensuring that we won't forget them. Every day, it brings us new reasons for feeling guilty. One morning, however, that feeling will be gone. Time will triumph, as it should.

★★★

"I don't think my mother was a happy little girl," wrote de Beauvoir. Except for the first ten years of her marriage, she explains, her mother had not known what is called *happiness* as a wife. What exactly is meant by that hazy word we have replaced with *desire*? Oddly enough, I never asked myself if my mother had been happy. Perhaps I was too self-centred, or too naïve, or I felt that she lived the life she had wanted.

A brief memory. I am seven or eight years old, there is no school, and I am rocking myself in the kitchen while my mother listens to her radio programs, Jovette Bernier's *Je vous ai tant aimés* and, right after, Professor Chentrier. He is a psychologist, I think, a kind of father-confessor. Women write to him, complaining about their husbands disappointing them, about their boring lives, and about their problems with their sisters-in-law. Théo Chentrier dispenses his advice in a patriarchal voice. He speaks well, he even has the accent of someone from France. And I, in my rocking chair, learn about life.

From Monday to Friday my mother takes a break from her chores to press her ear to the radio. This morning he replies to *her*. He has picked my day off, I'm lucky. Mama has sent him a letter. A woman presenter reads it. I only remember one sentence, "I am a happy woman." And Théo Chentrier praises her for being content with what she has. Happy women are few and far between! It is not so much a gift as a way of looking at things, a philosophy. I think that's what he says. It's what I understand, anyway.

I formed a picture of my mother from that single sentence, without puzzling over her need to hear a man on the radio confirm that she was happy. I might have wondered if she wasn't trying to hide something from herself. And what was *I* trying to hide from myself by simply believing her? Her mother's hysterectomy, her year-long stay at Nicolet, the Great Depression, her sister's illness, the four years in Toronto? Had all that not been difficult? And she got married at thirty-four, she must have had unhappy love affairs she never mentioned. She chose to draw a clear line between her life as a girl and that as a mother, "We are all entitled to our secrets." I was condemned to know only the woman who was my mother, but who can boast that they really know their parents?

My mother has not been spared. Yet my memory of her is that of a happy woman. I can't see her any other way. And I don't believe I'm deluding myself. She knew how to make the most of every moment, appreciating all she had been given. She didn't feel sorry for herself, and she never burdened her children with her misfortunes, great or small. She was neither depressive nor aggressive. She knew how to age well. It's a talent she had. Did she get it from her father, her mother, or was it simply her own? We never know exactly where *resilience*, as we now call it, comes from. Perhaps from her grandmother Émilie, whom she loved to talk about with me.

In the seventies, I mistook her strength for weakness. "We want the world and we want it now," Paul Chamberland reminded us at *La nuit de la poésie*. It was our slogan, we weren't a generation willing to be satisfied with a small life. I wanted to live life to the fullest—work, children, love affairs. I wanted to create, go to shows and movies, travel. I wanted an interesting, rich, exciting existence. In fact, by giving me an education, didn't my mother want that for me, too? So why was she satisfied with the way *she* lived?

"I have lived the life of the women of my generation," she would tell me. "The women of your generation are privileged." She didn't have the opportunities I had. In 1974, when women were coming into their own in Quebec, she turned sixty. It was too late. There were times when I detected regret in her voice. But not the devastating envy I encountered around me. Roadblocks, criticisms, tantrums, even spells of mental illness—some mothers would do anything to hold their daughters back. They couldn't accept being surpassed. *My* mother helped me along.

Mothers want their sons to achieve more than they have themselves. They expect it. They assign them that task. But the girls of my generation often felt that they were betraying their mothers, abandoning them. Little has been said about the guilt felt by daughters who pushed themselves to the limit to reach their full potential. When you combine education, work, children and creative pursuits, you cannot be as fully present to someone as when you lead a less busy life.

When I gave my mother my doctoral dissertation, she asked, "Did you read all those books?" A surprising, and moving, question. It was obvious, a doctorate required an enormous amount of work, books to be read and reread, research, months of thinking, writing, and living like a recluse. It had never occurred to me to explain it to her. She suddenly understood. She realized what had taken up my time and energy the previous years. She saw it wasn't a question of a lack of love for her. An educated daughter is what she had wanted, but there had been a price to pay.

Guilt didn't wreak havoc on me because my mother never tried to magnify it. She accepted that I lived my own life. She rarely criticized me for not visiting more often. But one evening, in the dimly lit living room, she told me, "When you get old, you have to get used to being alone." So it wasn't that easy for her. She wasn't unhappy, but happiness, as she understood it, was what she had in her earlier life, when we were all together in the old house on 1ère Avenue Nord. Now, she needed to force herself to feel joy, every day, as if it were an exercise program. The joy of simple things. Having us over for a visit, reading a novel she liked, stargazing at night from her glass doors. Telling herself that she was in good health. That her children, in spite of everything, were thinking of her.

★★★

If we had known that my mother had less than two months to live in November of 2011, would we have acted the way we did? There's no doubt we would have pretended everything was fine. She would have spent carefree days in her apartment until her body stopped by itself, on December 30th, like a worn-out machine.

Why, I often wonder, did I refuse to see the signs of her imminent end? It upsets me that I couldn't read reality, couldn't see the black shadow of death looming like the pitch-dark December nights gathering at the glass doors of the living room. Guilt, once again? Anxiety rather, for not having recognized it. I have felt that before with friends who suffered from cancer. Clear images come back to me. My aunt, who went to do her shopping as usual the day before a fatal coma. And that Czech friend who, as she lay dying, ordered the Russian nurse out of her room. My mother wasn't anywhere near that stage. She telephoned her friends, she laughed, enjoyed her food, and watched television. The social worker even talked about rehabilitation after the geriatric assessment. No one suspected that death was already doing its work. Why were we all so blind?

My mother chose to take advantage of every moment given to her. When we were children, she would serve us our meal and then sit down quietly, taking the time to eat and sip her tea afterwards while reading the paper. The dishes and the housework could wait. When she cooked supper, swept or vacuumed the floor, she would often stop to chat with Grandmother or listen to the radio. She liked to take breaks from her work, she did things at a leisurely pace. She was never obsessed with cleanliness. She didn't dust every day, and she allowed us to scatter our toys, never scolding us so we'd put them away. She wanted us to have fun. And we had a lot of fun.

During my teenage years, I would have liked her to dispatch her chores faster, the way it was done at my girlfriends' homes, where a clear line existed between pleasure and housework. Their mothers could sunbathe on the lawn, or take the afternoon off to go shopping or visit their friends. "I am slow," my mother would say. That annoyed me. I would have liked her to have free time, too. When she'd say with a laugh, "A housewife's work is never done," I felt like replying, "That's because you don't know how to go about it." She had married late. She had been used to the working world. She hadn't learnt to keep house at the age when young women acquired those skills. Later, I understood that my grandparents never made an issue of housework, just as my mother never insisted on it with me.

The truth, I believe, is that she loved family life. She attached the same importance to life's every gesture, every act, no matter how tiny—watching robins on the grass, stopping to talk to the woman next door while hanging out the washing, attending her vegetable garden, going to the market. She'd had enough of working in an office as an optician. Perhaps that is the reason why she never went back to work once she was married. In her deepest being, she enjoyed every moment of her days.

I had the good fortune of being brought up by a woman who wasn't dissatisfied with her life, unlike many other housewives of that period. Yet, in my teenage years, my mother's concerns seemed trivial to me. Her purchases at the market, the dishes she was going to cook for us, the clothes to be put away or taken out depending on the season, the mothballs in the wardrobes, housecleaning every week—that's what I would be able to escape by learning Latin and Greek. Actually, it wasn't these tasks that exasperated me, but the space they took up in one's head, space no longer available for knowledge. One had to make a choice between caring for the body and caring for the mind, between the world of women and that of men. You aren't born a woman, you become one—didn't Simone de Beauvoir set the example?

Later, when I read contemporary women writers, these two opposing poles were reconciled. One could take pleasure in cooking and enjoy teaching or writing as well. Marguerite Duras liked to cook her leek soup and would talk with Xavière Gauthier while making jam. Madeleine Gagnon painted Easter eggs for her sons. To have access to intellectual life, I didn't need to discard part of myself anymore. I could chat with my mother about cooking or sewing again, and value what had been the essence of her life. Is it possible to be solely a mind?

Thought germinates during the humblest activities—walking, the dishes, gardening, housework. That's what writers say. We sit in front of our screen, and our mind is a complete blank. There's no point in staying there all morning, it's better to go and do our shopping. Then, as we are buying cheese, a word occurs to us, or an idea. One could call it *writing without writing*. Without our knowledge, writing is creating a small space for itself within us. It waits for the right moment to emerge. When we go back to our desk the next day, the sentences will take shape almost by themselves. The project will have moved along without us noticing.

My mother was able to drop whatever she was doing to listen to a tune she liked on the radio, look at a painting, or touch a fabric. She loved beauty in all its forms, and strived for it in the dishes she cooked, the clothes she sewed, and the scarves she knitted for us. If she wasn't satisfied, she started over. Take that little kelly green coat, for example, she once made for my daughter from a left-over piece of material. The coat didn't suit the colouring of a brunette at all. "It will suit a blonde or a girl with light brown hair better," she had said, disregarding the hours of work she put in. And she gave it to a charity organization. She enjoyed making the coat, why would she regret having wasted her time? She would enjoy making another one. The result couldn't always meet her expectations. It was useless to get angry or discouraged.

She understood that long before I did.

★★★

On every page, my mother's portrait grows clearer. Or rather, I catch sight of a different image in the first one, as in anamorphoses. And I am forced to re-examine the picture of my childhood. My view changes constantly, no doubt because I can observe the woman she was from a greater distance, from every angle, without the irritations that are the fabric of the love between mother and daughter. I no longer have to compare myself to her or defend myself. Now we each inhabit our own planet.

The mother, life's most significant figure, the body in which we lived for nine months, the being that personifies love in all its perfection. We only need to take a moment and look at paintings of the Madonna and Child, the blissful smiles on the lips of the mother and her son. Love in all its glory. "That's amore," is a phrase I saw in a restaurant near my home. On the wall, a photograph of the owner with his wife and their four children. Right beside it, the negative had been cropped. Only the seven-or-eight-year-old son in front of his mother had been kept, with "That's amore" written next to it. All during the meal, I wondered if it was conceivable to have a similar picture of a mother and daughter. Wouldn't there be something unnatural, even obscene, about that?

For a daughter, it's a battle for femininity. The mother has to be both imitated and eclipsed, but she won't let her daughter steal her place so easily. "Mirror, mirror on the wall, who is the fairest of them all?" asks Snow White's stepmother, clearly seeing that the girl will soon replace her as winner in the attractiveness stakes. How old is Snow White? Sixteen, perhaps. And the stepmother? About thirty-five, the age at which a woman was already old at that time. The age at which my own mother gave birth to me. Today, many women have their first pregnancy in their late thirties. How does that affect the rivalry between mother and daughter? I wonder.

Accepting that Snow White is beautiful, more beautiful than *she*, requires a love for her child that a stepmother doesn't have. She may turn mean. A mother, on the other hand, is supposed to love her daughter unconditionally. But it isn't easy for a woman to see the first wrinkles furrowing her face, her body's muscles slackening. Not easy to notice she no longer exists in the male gaze. My mother must have experienced it. Yet I never sensed it. Was this a sign of love or maturity? Perhaps she considered herself *more mother than woman*, as Caroline Éliacheff and Nathalie Heinich put it. At least that was said about French Canadian women, who were actually called *Mother* by their husbands.

My father was no exception to the rule. I don't remember him ever calling my mother *Cécile*. She was the mother of the family and that included him, but this didn't prevent desire between them. They had an active sexual life. I found that out later through discreet hints. What I knew is that my father didn't look at girls. Orphaned at a very young age, he preferred motherly-looking, full-bodied women, as he used to say. My mother had her man, she didn't feel neglected in any way. She didn't have to compare herself with me. She hoped I would grow into a pretty, elegant, appealing young woman. By *her* standards, though. Deep down, a mother would like her daughter to become her double, whereas the daughter tries to distance herself enough from her mother so as not to resemble her.

There is always this struggle for independence on the part of the daughter, which reaches its critical moment in the teenage years, the difficult age. The separation is written in black and white in the relationship between mother and daughter. It has to happen and, like any separation, it gives rise to aggression, tears, outbursts, and anger. The more space for freedom opens up before us, the more these tensions will ease. But they will only end when the mother lets go for good. When she disappears.

It's since my mother died that I have been able to fully appreciate her.

★★★

There is all I haven't yet said about her, all I won't say, all I won't be able to capture. How could I conjure up her old, rasping voice that affected me so deeply when I telephoned her in the morning during those final months? And her bursts of laughter when she'd forget about the state of her health? And how stubborn she looked in the presence of the social worker, whom she mistrusted more than the police? And her love for her grandchildren? And for that great-grandson who happened to arrive when she had just broken her shoulder while stepping out of a taxi? In spite of her advanced age, she had recovered quickly. She hadn't had time to feel sorry for herself. Her young-mother concerns took over—the child's weight, the woollen socks to be knitted, colic and colds. It was real life, as in the old days.

In a photograph I had framed, she sits in her apartment on her old love seat, beside my daughter, and she is holding the newborn in her arms. A radiant smile. You would never believe this woman is ninety-three years old, never believe that a few weeks earlier, her arm was in a sling, her face full of bruises. The woman in the picture won't let herself go. She has just fallen head over heels in love with this child she enfolds for the first time, she wants to see him grow up. How can words truly convey that love?

"I alone know the exact shade of blue of the scarf the young woman wears in that book," wrote Marguerite Duras. And right now, only *I* am dazzled by my mother's enchantment on that day. It is the writer's constant struggle with language. We are unable to render exactly what we see, or hear, or feel, or touch. But we think we will succeed, we *want* to succeed, just as in her all-consuming passion the woman in the photo wants to live. We write because we long to share with others—our fellow human beings —what will only ever belong to ourselves. Naïveté or pride? Despondency, surely. Bereavement writing brings to mind the attitude of the great lyric poets who wanted to make their beloved eternal.

I took from my shelves all the books by daughters and sons who have written about their mother's death, and put them on the table. ...*et la nuit* by Anne-Marie Alonzo, *Journal de deuil* by Roland Barthes, *Une mort très douce* by Simone de Beauvoir, *La dernière leçon* by Noëlle Châtelet, *Le livre de ma mère* by Albert Cohen, *Ma mère et Gainsbourg* by Diane-Monique Daviau, *Pendant la mort* by Denise Desautels, *Dixhuitjuilletetdeuxmillequatre* by Roger DesRoches, *L'arrière-boutique de la beauté* by Fernand Durepos, *Je ne suis pas sortie de ma nuit* by Annie Ernaux, *Le deuil du soleil* by Madeleine Gagnon, *La petite mariée de Chagall* by Paul Chanel Malenfant, *La femme de ma vie* by Francine Noël, *Le temps qui m'a manqué* by Gabrielle Roy. What do I expect of them? A truth, consolation, an answer? But there will be no answer, no consolation, I know that.

    I won't let my mother rest in peace, beside my father, in their small cemetery. Beneath soothing intentions, this narrative is an act of refusal, of rebellion. I don't know if it will allow me to accept the loss. I don't know if writing can do that. This uncertainty does not kill my desire to write. My *need* to write, I should say. It arises from the depths of the body. Like eating or sleeping. Every morning I turn on my computer, I open the file I have called *My Mother*, I reread what I've written the previous day. And quietly my fingers start tapping away again, a word, a sentence, perhaps just a comma, then I erase, I move something, I move it back. It's silly, those thousands of tiny changes in the text, but I'm happy. For an hour or two I feel as if I am still with her, my very-much-alive mother, as when I telephoned her in the morning. I often think of a remark by Georges Didi-Huberman, "Isn't art perhaps what lets us imagine that the milk of our dead mothers—although the wound remains raw—still quenches our thirst?"

    One morning I will sense that this narrative is about to end. But that moment may never come, I may be tied to it until I die. Unlike in my fiction, where I can if not foresee then at least sense the way the story might end, I will never be able to exhaust my memory. A character exists only within the pages of a novel or a short story, but my mother will always be larger than this narrative in which I try to fit her. I will never have the last word. But I write. I carry on with the story while trying not to worry. I have to. It's a strange way of putting myself through my paces. There will be things left unsaid, I know, and ambiguity, vagueness. We will not see the blue of her scarf, or that of the blouse she made for herself from a remnant, or that of her linen summer suit, which I gave to a charity organization.

    I may not come to terms with the loss of my mother, but at

least I am slowly coming to terms with the loss of perfect writing that could give me back reality.

★★★

How can you describe the relationship between a mother and her child without falling back on platitudes? That's what I've been pondering since I saw *Tokyo Story* by Japanese filmmaker Ozu. I was moved to tears by that elderly couple who left their house in the care of their youngest daughter and set out on a long journey to visit their other children in Tokyo. But these children have neither the desire nor the time to look after their parents. Their presence bothers them. They ask a sister-in-law to take care of them, then pack them off to a fashionable thermal spa. The parents return unexpectedly. They are made to feel unwelcome. They decide to go home.

The mother dies shortly after her return. The children come, but go back to Tokyo as soon as possible after the funeral, without compassion for their father. Only the daughter-in-law takes the time to spend a few days with him. The one who gives, it so happens, is the one who receives nothing. Thoughtlessness? Ungratefulness of the children? Undeniably. Yet there is no moral in the film, only a portrayal of the facts. Children grow away from their parents and have their own lives. It's only natural, the daughter-in-law points out to the youngest daughter, who is outraged by her siblings' behaviour. If the father is disappointed, he doesn't show it.

There's a bit of the *Tokyo Story* children in all of us. My mother accepted that. It has been this way since children no longer needed to take care of their parents until they die. So why are we so eager to have children nowadays? Why are some women ready to resort to medically assisted procreation or adoption? Reproduction has been embedded deep in our genes and in our customs since the beginning of time, of course, but that answer doesn't completely satisfy me. My mind keeps circling around the mysterious force that drives us to procreate, even though the planet today is on the verge of collapsing under the weight of its inhabitants. Perhaps we dread ending up alone in the world.

The relationship between a mother and her child is one from cradle to grave. Friendships, ties of affection, attachments to people we like or feel close to, and love affairs don't last, as we well know. Not our whole lives. The bond with the mother is rooted in the first wails, the breastfeeding, the earliest ailments, the baby teeth. In our prehistory. It's indestructible, even in the presence of incomprehension, aggressiveness, or hatred. We can become indifferent to someone we loved, but never to our mother.

Our mother's death tears us permanently from our roots. She can no longer be held responsible for our happiness or despair. From then on, we have to take charge of our own destiny. I feel this, at the cemetery, one November afternoon, amid the fragrance of chrysanthemums.

★★★

She never got on a plane. Never saw the sea or the desert. Never went to Paris, as she would have liked to so much. I wanted to take her there after my father died, but she refused, she thought she was too old. It was no use pointing out to her that one could still travel at her age, as some of her friends proved. I wasted my time. At night, she would name the places she would never see. Notre-Dame Cathedral, the Eiffel Tower, the Champs-Élysées, the Louvre. "I'd rather dream about them," she'd say. She had chosen imagination over reality. It's hard to believe that during the war this woman left her home town to go and live in Toronto for four years. She came back from there to get married.

For me, as a child, Toronto was a vast city with a streetcar, an office of American Optical where my mother had worked, an Eaton's store, and Protestant churches. But there were also Catholic churches where you could meet French-speaking people on Sunday. And there was Marguerite, a Québécoise my mother met there. And Colette, a French-speaking woman from Sudbury with whom Mama lived until Colette's husband came back from the war. And Betty and Sydney, who rented out a room to her. At Christmastime they sent us presents, and my mother mailed presents to them, too, for their children. She was especially attached to Douglas, the oldest. She must have longed to have a little boy like him someday. Barbara was born the year she got married.

Betty used to enclose black-and-white photographs in her parcels. Mama would examine them with narrowed eyes. "Betty doesn't change," she'd say. Or, "She has lovely children." Our Quebec cousins hadn't played with us for a long time, they were married. We were thrilled to have cousins our own age in Toronto. I knew they weren't my real cousins, but they belonged to the family because Mama said so. In the word *family*, you could put all the people you loved, even if they spoke another language, even if they weren't of the same religion as us.

My mother knew lots of English-speaking people in Sherbrooke. Friends, old classmates, or women she used to work with. And we said hello to our Italian neighbour every day, also to another neighbour, a Portuguese woman Mama was fond of. If they weren't part of the family, it was because they didn't give us presents at Christmastime, but nothing prevented us from liking them. Was that attitude characteristic of our town or only of my mother? I don't know. Her four years in Toronto certainly opened up new horizons for her.

But my mother's affection for Toronto, for the people she spent time with there, was separate from her political convictions. She immediately subscribed to René Lévesque's vision, and his death was a shock for her. She had lost a member of her family, of her political family this time. She never really got over that loss—she began to have doubts. In the last year of her life, she would ask me while watching the television news in her rocking chair, "Do you still believe Quebec will be independent?"

The world had changed. Her children travelled more and more. They'd visit her with friends from Europe or South America. She was getting used to seeing her grandson go off to Africa for his work. She regularly called her other grandson in China. While hanging up, she'd say, "When I was young, only missionaries went to live there." The planet was now at the end of her white receiver, she couldn't get over it. What did she really think? She greeted the change as an established fact, a certainty one needed to get used to. Cultivating nostalgia was pointless. But her regrets would resurface some evenings in the dimly lit living room, and then she'd say with a quaver in her voice, "Those were the days."

Those days shifted for her from one period to another depending on the conversation, but they were always connected with her life as a married woman. They sometimes included the days when we were children, or teenagers, at other times the years when she looked after her grandchildren, or when my father was still alive, or else those when Quebec buzzed with excitement. I never heard her say, "Those were the days," when she spoke about her childhood or her stay in Toronto. She enjoyed telling us about the mischief she got into with her cousins in Nicolet, her strolls down Yonge Street, and the visit from her uncle Arthur to the office in Toronto, who had caused quite a stir with his raccoon coat.

She didn't appear wistful about those stages in her life. It was as though they belonged to a predetermined time, clearly bordered by a beginning and an end. But it seemed abnormal to her that her children and grandchildren had grown up, that my father was dead, and René Lévesque also. The house, Sherbrooke, and

Quebec were Russian dolls to her—they fit into one another, and were part of the same protected reality, unlikely to plunge into the abyss. She didn't really care about Paris, the calm sea of Cuba, the large waves of the Pacific, the Sahara, or dry Arizona. The blue bird was in her garden, as in the story.

"You travel for me," she'd say when we were getting ready to go off somewhere, relieved she didn't have to pack. The more time passed, the more it was a wrench for her to leave her apartment, even for a few hours, she tried to explain to me. As if a disaster might occur in her absence. What vise had slowly fastened around her? She must have noticed the puzzled look on my face because she immediately added, "You'll understand when you'll be as old as I am." But it happened long before, it happened with her marriage, with the birth of her children. She didn't travel anymore, except to Montreal or Saint-Antoine, when we'd go to our uncles' places. She never returned to Toronto.

I collect names of people who stayed active even in extreme old age—Jean Rouch, Simone de Beauvoir, Claire Martin, Raymond Klibansky, Nathalie Sarraute. Teachers, intellectuals, artists, writers. People who had a passion. But such lives are out of bounds for the vast majority of people, especially mothers. How do we avoid closing ourselves off?

Motherhood remains the cornerstone of femininity, the place where theories confront reality, ideals encounter life's ups and downs, and the needs of the child meet the limits of the mother. We never come out of it unscathed. We will always feel a pang of sadness when we choose ourselves at the detriment of our child. But never putting ourselves first will inevitably lead to a narrowing of our horizons. What kind of balance can we find between the love for ourselves and the love for a child?

A WOMAN OF HER TIME

★★★

A week after his mother died, Roland Barthes wrote in his diary: "Many people still love me, but from now on my death wouldn't kill any of them—and that's what is new." This entry disturbed me, no doubt because my own death or that of my brothers would not have killed our mother. Was Barthes loved more than we were? Did his mother have less fortitude than ours? Or is there an obligation in my family to come to terms with grief? An obligation or permission?

Every time Great-grandmother Émilie lost a child, she shut herself up in her room to cry and she would stay alone up there for as long as she needed to. Then she dried her tears and took up her life where she left it. She didn't talk about her child anymore, I was told. And I would picture Émilie coming down the stairs in her long black dress, red-eyed, but with her handkerchief now tucked into her sleeve. It was more than an anecdote, it was the lesson Émilie had passed on to Léda, then Léda to my mother, and then to me.

Roland Barthes' admission is one Albert Cohen could have made as well, in the light of his mother's love for him. But could a woman? In mythology, Demeter does not recover from Hades' abduction of her daughter Persephone, but she doesn't kill herself for all that. She gets Zeus to agree to let her daughter come back and spend nine months of the year with her. During those other months, Persephone will stay in the Underworld, with her husband. A give-and-take solution. Those involved learn to share. The goddesses seem satisfied. Living together twelve months of the year would have been impossible. Can a woman have as symbiotic a relationship with her mother as a man?

Barthes never left his mother. Their love was akin to adulation well beyond the sexual relationship between a man and a woman. Barthes wrote on October 27, 1977: "You have never known a woman's body?—I have known the body of my sick, and then dying, mother." A woman will say she looks after her sick mother as after a child. She becomes the mother of her mother. Here, we are in the presence of a passionate relationship. Both mother and son were incapable of facing the other's death.

In order to come to terms with the loss of our mother, shouldn't we first acknowledge that she would have survived our own death? The truth is that we weren't everything to her. She had a husband, other children, friends. She wasn't constantly interested in the little girl we were. She took care of herself, of what *she* wanted, as well. The sorrow of death makes us relive thirty, forty, sixty or even seventy years of major and minor infidelities. Major and minor humiliations. With the sorrow and the anger, we cannot avoid grief.

"Go and play by yourself. I have other things to do." Better, more urgent, more important things? We don't ask, we don't want to know. We put balm on the wound as best we can. In an hour, it will reopen anyway. We'll be confronted once again with cruel reality. Is it conceivable that a mother never hurt her son? Or are there sons who have such an intensely close relationship with their mother that they don't feel these hurts? In that case the death of the mother is a hardship they won't recover from.

We weren't everything to our mother. And she wasn't everything to us. The thought causes a pang of sadness, but then the feeling changes, and we suddenly become lighter, we laugh, we sing while listening to music. We dance, cook a nice meal, drink a Campari and Soda. We make love as when we were twenty, play with our grandson, stroke the cat, go to the theatre or the movies. We want to see the latest exhibition at the museum, explore the world. We intend to be happy again.

We briefly forget our mother, and we feel happy. We picture a woman of the late nineteenth century, like Émilie, at the very moment she leaves her room, steps into the corridor, then heads down the stairs that take her to the kitchen, with reddened eyes, but with her handkerchief tucked into the sleeve of her long black dress.

★★★

Great-grandmother Émilie was like a character from a novel. My mother would describe her to me in elaborate detail—her long black dress, her little white collar. Then there was Great-grandfather Louis, and the old three-storey family home, her unmarried daughters Alexandrine and Rosa who helped her keeping house, and the town of Nicolet with its cathedral, its seminary, the priests and the nuns. And the baker, Monsieur Toupin, the pork and beans he used to cook in his oven for Sunday morning, and Great-grandmother's accent, which my mother imitated with a laugh.

Would my mother have liked to write? I am sure it was never a dream of hers. But she had given a talk on the radio one day, she told me with rosy cheeks, a talk on Madame de Sévigné. I was struck dumb with admiration. Why Madame de Sévigné? Chance, a commission, her own wish? What if *she* had had a passion for women's writing before *me*? If she had written, she would have become a novelist, I'm sure. I tried several times to take her along to public readings I was a part of in Sherbrooke, just to get her out of her apartment. She would pull a face—poetry didn't interest her. And yet my grandfather read local poets. Mama always spoke to me about that with pride. She also admired Jovette Bernier, who lived on rue King, near 1ère Avenue. And Alfred DesRochers. So it was *my* poetry that didn't interest her. To spare myself, I never asked her why.

I guessed the truth. It is difficult for a family to have a child who writes, who writes in a literary genre close to autobiography, as is the case with poetry. My mother must have taken quite a beating when my first poetry collection, *La peau familière*, was published. Even though I had taken refuge behind certain complex, contemporary constructions, she knew how to read—I talked about my background, how difficult I found it to live, she had understood very well what I meant. After thinking about it, she said, "If you really think that, you did well to write it." And we never talked about it again. Deep down, she must have envied her good friend Mariette, who was lucky enough to have a visual artist for a son. Nothing about the family showed up in his works.

I, too, often envied M.G. for being able to carry on with his work without having to ask himself at every installation, every exhibition, if his family might be upset. I should have chosen another art—painting or music. Like several other people, I took up writing because writing didn't cost anything. There is always paper and there are always pencils in even the most modest families, always books you can borrow from the library. And there was a university in Sherbrooke where you could study literature.

The writer in the family is the one who can cause a scandal. In our home there was no murder, no incest, no fraud, no money laundered and deposited in tax havens. Only life, life that leaves scars we don't want to reopen. It is impossible to write if we don't venture into the heart of what made us. I have always gone forward like a tightrope walker on the wire of poetry. Hurt my mother's feelings, *that's* what I didn't want to do. Her death would free me, I used to think. I was wrong. Even though she is dead, she is still my mother. She will be my mother for all eternity.

It was when my first novel came out that I became a writer in her eyes. "Your book," she would proudly say to me, as if I hadn't had anything published before. The figure of the writer is that of the novelist, as we know. The novel requires less effort from the reader than poetry, and there are characters—we can decide to silence any autobiographical suspicion. My mother always chose to read my novels as works that sprang directly from my imagination, even when events from the past were barely disguised.

When *La Voie lactée* was published, I asked her if she had been moved by certain scenes. She didn't answer, she came back to the plot right away, I had written a beautiful love story, a man and a woman who believe in life. I gave up with a sense of relief. It was cowardly of me no doubt, but my mother had just given me a good excuse to stop worrying. Perhaps that's what she wanted anyway. She had grown used to the idea that I wrote, and from time to time my picture appeared in the newspaper. Her friends would call her, I was her daughter after all, I wasn't a disgrace to her. Isn't it better to have a daughter who writes than a daughter who holds up banks? I often jokingly said that to myself to make myself feel better.

But we never feel better for good. *Tout comme elle*, in 2006, caused my anxiety to resurface. I had drawn my inspiration from my reading, from confidential talks, from what I had observed, but I, too, had a mother. I couldn't disregard that, and certain elements of our relationship, trivial ones at times, shone through. Fortunately, my mother didn't want to come and see the play in Montreal. It was too far, too tiring. And I didn't give her the book. Some scenes are harsh, the one for example where the daughter is bored in the company of her old mother, where her bones creak from boredom. I can't deny having been bored once in a while. But in the text such a brief spell is magnified. It's a feature of the theatre that it turns a detail into a dramatic event.

A few months later, I found out that she had ordered the book at a bookstore near her home. Comparing her name with mine, the bookseller had asked her if we were related. "That's my daughter," she'd said. She thought fit to tell me. Had she been upset, had she wondered if I loved her, if she had been a good mother? I couldn't bring myself to ask her straight out. I explained to her that it was fiction, as in novels, and that the text moved through all the stages of the separation of mother and daughter—love, angry outbursts, reconciliations. I don't know if she believed me. She changed the subject, as usual, and I just sat there, repeating a sentence from *Tout comme elle* to myself, "I have never known how to talk to her."

Like my mother, I don't know how to talk. Who passed that down to us? Léda, my grandmother, or Émilie, or her mother, or the mother of her mother? I can only speculate. I may have written books so I could talk to my mother about the things I was unable to tell her. About the things she didn't want to hear. And now that she is gone, perhaps I seek her ear through my readers.

★★★

There is a magical sun today despite the intense cold. I hear my mother's hoarse voice on the telephone again, "If only you could see the beautiful blue sky!" From my ground-floor home, all I saw were cars parked on my street, but from her fifth-floor apartment, she was able to admire the sky. I think calmly about my mother. No lump in my throat, no flinching. I have grown used to thinking of her as someone who is dead. I am now well and truly used to her death.

Perhaps it's because my love for my mother was commonplace, lacklustre. I am ashamed, I am not worthy of the dazzling sunshine in the window, not worthy of my mother. She deserved better than me. It is said that once grief has been dealt with, we are left with a peaceful memory, but I wish my soul was raw again. I miss the sorrow of the first months of grieving, the sorrow that kept my mother alive and kept me alive in the life of my mother, as when I was a child. The exultation of all-consuming sorrow that won't let go. But I am detached from my mother now, I am grown-up, responsible, an adult, how sad.

I am sad that I am no longer sad. It would be enough to make you laugh, but I don't have a sense of humour. All isn't lost, then. All isn't lost because the slightest sunshine in the morning makes me think of my mother. Or, rather, the thought comes to me unbidden, it makes its way, imposes itself. And for a few brief moments I am at peace with myself, I am not the fickle, inconsiderate woman I believed I had become, I have a good image of myself again. I don't need to worry, my past still exists, my past still moves me. I don't feel cut off from myself. I am not dead. But I know now that *my mother* is dead. I no longer say to myself, "I'm going to tell Mama about this." I no longer think of giving her a call.

Nonetheless, a hole is forming in my head, an empty space that grows and grows. I feel it, it can't fill up again. I am forgetting things. Small, trivial things, to send an email, take clothes to the cleaner's, pay the taxes. I drift along on the line of human time, I travel between birth and death, between my mother's past and my own future. I try to come to grips with the idea of my own end. Will I be able to count on a long life, I wonder? A feeling of urgency, I may have only a few years left to write, to bear witness, to pass on what is important to me. What will that be? I don't know. Do we ever know what we are going to pass on?

Is this feeling of drifting a stage of normal grieving? I couldn't care less. I couldn't care less to find out if I am normal, if I react according to the books. I'm afraid of sinking into forgetfulness. It's at my age that Alzheimer's begins. Yesterday I forgot my cellphone number. And I kept telling myself, "It doesn't matter." I am still able to think about my mother, the way she was just before she died. That isn't such a distant memory. Only a year.

I say *forgetfulness*, but it isn't the right word. The truth is that I take no interest in everyday life. I just can't concentrate on boring tasks or ordinary conversations with my neighbours. I can't remember what I'm reading, I have to go back to the beginning of an article or a poem. I may be suffering from attention deficit disorder, I always had my head in the clouds in primary school. So I am lapsing into my second childhood. It worries me but doesn't depress me. A friend said to me recently regarding my mourning, "You seem to be managing well." I told her, "I was prepared." And right away I felt stupid. Can you be prepared for the death of your mother? You expect it, but you are never prepared for it.

I am thinking of my mother. In the first months after she died, I kept saying, *I am thinking of you, Mama*, as if she were still among us. The slightest object that had belonged to her brought her back to life, her old sewing machine, a woollen blanket, the cup I drank my coffee from whenever I went to see her in Sherbrooke. Gradually the sewing machine, the woollen blanket, and the cup took their place in my home. It no longer surprises me to see them there every morning. Now my thoughts have no address, I think of my mother as of someone who is not there.

All the same, I can see her nose, her black eyebrows, her smile, the bluish rivulets criss-crossing her hands. I hear her hoarse voice on the phone in the morning, when she hadn't talked to anyone yet, and her clearer evening voice in the dimly lit living room. I remember the expressions she liked to use, her dreamy look when she reminisced about her childhood. I can see her and hear her, but now, in order to tell stories about her, I have to make an effort to link the images together, to connect the words. I can still put her in brief scenes, but I am no longer able to give my mother a real presence, as in a home movie. Is it possible to lose one's mother forever? Is that what *nevermore* means?

I have the awful feeling that my narrative will end not because there will be nothing left to say about my mother, but because all that will come to me is the word *nevermore*. One intensely cold morning, I will hear "If only you could see the beautiful blue sky." I will recognize my mother's hoarse voice on the phone and I will think of her as if she were a stranger.

And I will see myself as a stranger, too. Perhaps I am one already.

***

Suddenly it's there, unchanged, that feeling I used to have when I went to sleep at my mother's apartment in Sherbrooke, in the small bedroom she reserved for her children and grandchildren. The feeling that nothing could happen to me under the heavy blankets my grandmother had woven by hand. I felt protected. And I slept as in my childhood bed. It was a miracle every time. I would wonder why I slept so peacefully while my mother grew more and more frail. In the morning, as I opened my eyes, I would say to myself, "These days will end soon."

Until now, I hadn't thought about those moments of serenity. In the final weeks of my mother's life, when her apartment needed to be kept at a high temperature, I had replaced the woollen blankets with cotton sheets and didn't sleep as soundly anymore. My mother would get up at night, and I had to make sure she didn't fall. The image of that old woman behind her walker in the darkness in her threadbare pink nightgown took up all the space in my memory. But now my earlier memories come back. There are advantages, it would appear, to seeing my mother as absent once and for all.

Because before—before her memory failed, before she told the same story a hundred times, before her cardiovascular incident, her difficulty walking, our growing concern—she enjoyed basking in the sweet things of life, in pleasure. Modest, quiet pleasure. She enjoyed eating, drinking her tea, reading her newspapers, doing her crossword puzzles, gazing at trees, looking for four-leaf clovers. She liked sheets that smelt of lavender, warm baths, and walks along the Rivière Saint-François. With her, I admired maples or willows, and riveted my eyes on the ground the moment I spotted a clump of clover. And yet I would feel uneasy, almost guilty. I should have been using that precious time for my tasks, correcting assignments, reading a master's thesis, writing a paper.

The following day, in the bus that took me back to Montreal, I returned to work, no longer anxious. The students, the lectures, the articles, the meetings—I was always snowed under with work. I was important in other people's lives. The thought of having nothing to do one day frightened me. I knew what my mother meant when she said, "One wants to feel useful," even though she valued pleasure. My mother worked until the age of thirty-four, raised three children, took care of her mother until she died, and then her grandchildren during holidays—she had difficulty accepting that no one needed her anymore.

Although over ninety, she continued to run small errands for her friends, going to the bank with them or the doctor. "I am still able to help others," she cheerfully told me on the phone on those nights. Then, little by little, the friends ended up in the hospital or the funeral home, she didn't venture out as often and, since her shoulder fracture, we wanted her to stay as close as possible to her apartment. *She* would need *us* from now on. She was aware of that, and felt humiliated.

"If you knew how hard it is to be constantly dependent on others," a paraplegic friend confided to me one evening. That's exactly what my mother felt at the core of her being. To the end, she rebelled when one of us cooked, washed the dishes, or put away food. She, who had never tolerated us in her kitchen, had no choice anymore, we no longer obeyed her. She wasn't taken in by the little ruses we employed to keep her busy during these small chores. Growing old means losing your independence and submitting to your children's will. Even if those children are acting in good faith, can you really ever accept that?

Now and then in those last years, she would talk about old age. It was not a decline for her. She had almost no pain, though her fingers grew more and more crooked. But she would show me her face, her arms, her stomach. She wore a scarf to hide her withered neck, she couldn't understand women who sunbathed in swimsuits by the residence's swimming pool.

No. Old age was not a decline, not a shipwreck, but a gradual humiliation, a loss of one's sense of self, which, while it couldn't be stopped, needed to be delayed. What I long considered to be a denial by my mother, I now see as an act of trickery. Pretending, not admitting you are losing your strength, that's what you might call *ageing wisely*. In order to live to a ripe old age, shouldn't we refuse to let go? Defy common sense, against all logic?

My mother possessed that fierce determination. Did she pass it on to me? I won't know until I hear that small voice urging me one day to give in to the obvious. My mother used cunning as long as she could, but when she ended up before the great black wall one frigid December night, she didn't struggle. She let herself slip into her final sleep.

★★★

My mother's death throes. In the silent darkness of a room at the end of the corridor. As for my father, he crossed the abyss one evening in May. It had been a dazzling day, sunshine, a mildness in the air, birds. The twilight, I remember, was something straight out of a travel brochure. To die suddenly on such an evening? The Grim Reaper turns up at any time, but I didn't learn my lesson. My mother was in the best of health then, she promised us to live to a greater age than her grandmother Émilie. And she kept her word, she lived five years longer than her. And twenty-five years longer than my father.

My father and my mother belonged to two distinct planets. I sensed that clearly when I was very small. Education, speech, manners, the way they dressed. My mother came from a cultured home environment, whereas my father had been left to his own devices. No one was to blame, only the cruelty of fate, the bad medicine of those days that let mothers die, the orphanage, the hard work on farms, the lack of love, the lack of care, the lack of everything. A melodramatic childhood. But my father never complained. He barely told us he had been beaten so hard at the orphanage one time that he couldn't sit down for quite a while. How old was he then? I don't know much about my father, before he became my father, I mean.

My mother had separated the present from the past. My father now had a wife, a house, children—he should let bygones be bygones. She always supported him, defended him. She loved him. I understood my mother's love for my father when an acquaintance of hers came to see her. The woman went on and on about her many trips, the presents her husband had given her, the seaside holidays, the big cars, everything my mother never had. When the woman asked her a question about her husband, my mother got my father's photograph from her bedroom and held it out to the visitor, who then exclaimed, "He really was a handsome man." My mother took the picture back, looked at it dreamily for a few moments. She hadn't travelled, she could never take her children to the seaside, she hadn't had big cars, but she had lived with a handsome man. She'd had the most important thing.

My mother told me with a laugh one night in the dimly lit living room that the essential thing for a couple was desire. One could come to terms with everything else. We still believe this today. She was prepared for the Quiet Revolution's upheaval in matters of love. She never blamed me at the times of my separations. My father did. *He* believed in marriage. He continued to go to Mass even when my mother no longer went, sometimes to Evening Prayer. When we lived in the old house on 1ère Avenue Nord, he would withdraw to the dining room to say his rosary. I felt more and more distant from him.

Women have generally shown themselves to be more open to new ideas than men. Ideas like cohabitation, separation, abortion, homosexuality. I have often noticed this around me. No doubt because they were closer to their children, and wanted that to continue at all costs. My father had his beliefs, but he didn't act the patriarch, he didn't forbid me to go out in the evening or go camping with friends. I was getting ready at one time to go away for a few days with my boyfriend when he said to me, "Be careful, don't come back pregnant." We had old parents, but they behaved better with us than many other parents who were younger than they. They agreed on how to bring us up.

Desire, and their view of their children's upbringing, that's what drew them together. But not just that. Current political events as well, which they followed with a passion. The news on the radio morning, noon, and night, and then the television news when an Admiral set entered the living room. That was in 1960. The neighbours had owned one for many years, but my parents insisted on paying cash. They were afraid of buying on credit. "One never knows," my mother used to say, images of the Great Depression still vivid in her mind. What she didn't say, no doubt because she wouldn't admit it to herself, was that my father might fall ill. Again. In spite of some minor health problems, he was fortunately able to work up to his retirement.

We were careful with money at home, but that didn't stop my mother from welcoming my friends, from having them stay for a meal. She liked people, my father did too. They even had one of my friends who had become depressed spend several days with us. My mother almost looked upon our chums as her own children. She consoled their heartbreaks, encouraged the ones who had family problems. The mood was joyful in our home. All these images came back to me at the funeral—so many friends from our childhood and teenage years were there, with the feeling that they, too, were burying a distant past.

"If you could have seen all the people at my grandmother's funeral in Nicolet!" my mother used to say to me. She got her friendliness from her. Émilie had fed boarders of the preparatory seminary for decades, as a way to supplement the family income at a time when women didn't work outside the home. The memory of Émilie came back to me during the funeral service, my mother would have been delighted to see all the people who had turned up for her. It was a final tribute to what she had accomplished. Just like her grandmother.

Before, when my mother was alive, I never tried to connect the threads of the present to those of the past. Now, I can spot more clearly the fragments I took from her. And the ones I couldn't take, and those I didn't want. But invisible bits exist as well, fragments I don't recognize, and never will. The ones I get from my grandmother, my great-grandmother—words, gestures, attitudes of a line of women going back to time immemorial. But also from her father, Bruno, and his lineage. There is all that I will never know about what passes through me.

But I am also my father's child. I carry pieces of him inside me. I have never asked myself what those might be. Perhaps because my father was cut off from his ancestors. I never knew his mother, Louisa. When I was born, my mother said to him, "We will call her Louise, like your mother." He agreed. Louise, like his mother. I descend as well from a woman who left five children behind, a dead woman whose face my father no longer remembered. Now I would like to find out who my grandmother Louisa was, and my grandfather Toussaint, and their mothers whose very names are unknown to me. And there is all I will never know about Léda, Émilie, Octavie. And Bruno. For me, my mother was a bulwark against the void. Now her death reveals a vast hole that will never be filled.

In a novel, I would be able to give a shape to Louisa. I would fantasize. I would write that my father was delighted that I carry his mother's name. He saw her come back to life in me. He recognized me as his child. But I am not writing a novel. This is a narrative of silence. The silence of all that has gone astray, been lost, forgotten in the memory of the generations. The silence of secrets as well. I write with my eyes riveted on what will forever be in darkness. I strive to hear the slightest sentence again, the most ordinary reply, as though I were listening to a tape I wanted to transcribe with perfect accuracy. I let those words slowly make their way within me. I try to interpret them. I become the exegete of a text full of holes passed down by my mother.

But she also revealed herself by her gestures, her facial expressions, the way she acted, the way her voice would quiver, her tears, her laughter. I always underestimated that silent speech, even though I came to writing through the theatre. I try to understand what she was saying when she frowned, when her face took on a dreamy look, when she didn't finish her sentences. To understand what she wanted to say to me when she was desperately trying not to say anything.

I now accept I'll have to struggle with those shadow zones I will never be able to throw light on. I will just have to live with what I'll never know about my mother or my father, with what I'll never know about myself. I try to adopt that line by Saint-Denys Garneau I never understood: "It is there, unsupported, that I rest." Could the end of mourning be the feeling that one can live unsupported from then on?

★★★

Between my mother and me, a bond is broken for ever. That is death. I wish I had known her better. I still try to pin words on what she didn't tell me, as though she could be returned to me, body and soul. The silences of this narrative have nothing to do with the inexpressible that lives in a poem. Here, nothing, no music, no song to transform grief, if only for a couple of lines. As I struggle with the powerlessness of language to bring my mother back to life, grief patiently continues on its way.

Wouldn't a poem harbour the secret dream of regaining the body-to-body intimacy with her, of denying the original separation? Poetry could meet my need for consolation, but not this narrative, not this narrative which confronts me continually with my mother's irrevocable death, and which will confront me with it until the last letter of the last word. What will there be at the end of this story? No consolation or understanding. Just the ability to live with the abyss at my back, without distress or anguish. Then I will admit that my mother's story is finished, and part of mine along with it. In a way, this book is the construction of my own grave.

But unlike Christ, I will not rise from the dead. What will happen is something infinitely small, infinitely humble. A shedding, or regeneration, like earthworms that can regrow after they are cut in half. Pieces of me do not hold as well as they used to. It's a strange sensation. Will they come off on their own? Or will I have to amputate myself? I don't know who I'll become. But I'm not afraid, I belong to a grief-stricken lineage, an age-old lineage of men and women who walk towards their death and feel it in the depths of their being.

To acknowledge that we are mortal is to peer out of the corner of our eye at the hole that will receive us, to measure the time we are still away from it. We are forced to ask ourselves what is important for the remainder of our lives. Writing, travelling, love?

Several people around me have found love after their mother died, others ended lukewarm relationships. There are women who decided to bear children. Our mother's death is an electric shock that can paralyse us or urge us on.

I choose to look ahead of me. It's what my mother would have done. But in the brain, borders are porous—all it takes is an old wound resurfacing, or a wave of nostalgia, for the past to awaken. Mourning, you could say, is like that game I played so often as a child. Snakes and Ladders. If you land on the square of the snake, you go down. But there are ladders, too, and in the end you arrive at the top, *In heaven*. That's what they said when I was little. So, we won't find peace until we die?

I have begun to be aware of time slowly wreaking its havoc. Stiffer fingers, more frequent medical examinations, memory lapses. That's only the beginning. The process, I know, is irreversible. "We fall apart," says my doctor, who is also in his sixties. I wonder if my mother felt it at that age, even though she didn't talk about it. She must have. She had lost her parents, she had arrived on the front line, she knew the sequence of things. In her eighties, she often said, "Life flies by! You are young and, suddenly, you are old."

Soon it will be my turn to say those words. I try to stop the years, but they slip away from me, and I have to run, I run faster and faster. Sometimes I picture myself at a convent, or in the desert, or in a tower by the sea. I spend my days contemplating the light, the minutes going by. I regain power over time. Then the present re-emerges. Small and stupid. A telephone call, a letter to write, a bill to pay, and I leave my reveries behind. If mourning cuts a notch between the past and the present, reality brings us back to the unbroken line of sightless days. *I* will be old, too, without having seen life fly by. And, like all the living, I will fight my last battle when I die. No mourning process will ever be able to ease my own death.

Does mourning help us to accept defeat? I am not a bit like Zorba the Greek—I would never be able to dance while my dream falls apart. I still see my mother in her rocking chair, outlined against her deep silence, those last weeks before she died. "It's no fun," she would say while thinking of what awaited her. She would look at me for a moment, then lower her eyes and fall silent. I remember famous people making jokes on their deathbed. Life cannot end with a witticism. That is unacceptable to me. Unless people are so intent on enhancing the very last impression they make that they are no longer capable of rational thought.

What was the final image in my mother's mind? Did scenes from the past still surface in her deep morphine sleep? I would like to believe she saw us all gathered around her to celebrate another New Year's Day. Or, for a brief moment, was she with my father again, as in their picture taken in 1948 in Toronto, before their marriage, when they walked along side by side, in love? Or had she gone back to her childhood, with her mother and father, her little sister, her dolls, or to Nicolet, with her grandmother? But an impenetrable cloud, as impenetrable as the night of that 30th of December, must have slowly surrounded her, since she died without complaining, moaning, or suffering.

Under the effect of morphine, we are robbed of our death, but what solution is there to be found to that dreadful reality unless we have our eye on eternal life? Some believe in cryogenics. My mother wouldn't have wanted that. She often said, "When it's over, it's over." And I agree with her. Life is worth it if you live it with the people you love. I wouldn't want to reappear two centuries later in a totally foreign, perhaps infernal, world. I have no confidence in our ability to evolve.

Death is still the best solution for those who lack unconditional faith in humanity.

For the past three days, Montreal has been ethereally white. Tree branches bend under the snow. Cars huddle along the sidewalks. Only the main roads have been cleared. Even on foot, it's difficult to get about. And people are shovelling endlessly. This time last year I was on the road with my brother from Terrebonne. We were coming back from Quebec City, still in a state of shock. My mother had just died. I thought about her all day yesterday, hour after hour, almost obsessively, and this morning too, from the moment I woke up. My arrival at the hospital, how sad I felt seeing her in the white bed, the waiting, the doctor's visit, the beginning of the long vigil, peritonitis setting in and morphine being given, relief, sleep, then eternal rest. A year ago now. I find it hard to believe.

    J.-P. and I have decorated a tree. We have added the three wooden panels to the hundred-year old dining-room table I brought back from Sherbrooke. I have prepared a turkey, green peas, mashed potatoes. There are also tourtières, rolls, a dish with olives and beets. My daughter made the ketchup we have been eating since we were small. For just one day, I would like my mother to be given back to us. But will copying the meal she cooked for sixty years be enough to bring her back to life?

    Eleven o'clock. Last year, she was waiting at the hospital mortuary. A hearse would go and pick her up in Quebec City. She had been dead for nearly nine hours. It was bitterly cold. On the road, we watched the scenery slip by the window. We didn't say much, my brother and I. I was trying to sort out the events of the past two days. My chat with my mother on Skype. She was fine, she smiled when she saw my old cat, she always loved cats. Then, just a few minutes later, a phone call from my brother in Quebec City. Suddenly Mama had begun to experience a lot of pain, he had asked for an ambulance. They would take her to the hospital. And the waiting, with the phone within reach, the bad news, it was pointless to operate on her, we needed to resign ourselves to the worst. And the hurried packing, the setting off for Quebec City.

I am expecting my family. I look out of the window. I hope some of the neighbours have dug their cars out of the snowdrifts. I hope everyone can find a place to park. I worry, just as my mother worried so often about the bad weather on New Year's Day. We will all be together without her. To celebrate the New Year or commemorate the first anniversary of her death? What will prevail, sadness or joy? I hear my mother's phrase again, "We mustn't let ourselves go." We'll follow her example. We'll practice being joyful once more. Like Marie-Amanda, in *Le Survenant*, when, as Christmas Eve dinner is about to begin, she seats her daughter at the now empty place of her mother, Mathilde Beauchemin. Because when "a leaf falls from the tree, another takes its place," Germaine Guèvremont concluded. It is nature's ruthless law and, despite all our knowledge, we humans can't escape it.

Marie-Amanda and I are worlds apart. She worked in the house without ever stopping even while pregnant with her third child. I would be incapable of living the life of that woman born in the late nineteenth century like Léda and Louisa, my two grandmothers. Yet she is the one I look to for support today. Over the years, I have constructed an imaginary family for myself, characters from novels or movies, writers who left phrases on which to reflect along my way.

Beyond the window, the maple is as stiff as a corpse. It's hard to imagine that it rustled with leaves last summer, that other leaves will take their place in the spring. But, fortunately, it will come back to life. It is "death with life inside," as Madeleine Gagnon wrote on the subject of Mozart's *Exultate, Jubilate*. That's what I want today, to conjure life from death itself, to rouse it, cultivate it, and see it unfold in tiny pleasures, smells, flavours, gestures, laughter, love. Aren't we programmed for life, like all species?

I now craft life from nothing, in spite of sadness, sadness with joy inside. Joy to resist the strong winds that carry away everything in their path. Even us. But do we have to start dying before death? I don't want my awareness to restrain me. I want to keep my enthusiasm, my energy, my ability to get back on my feet. Like my mother. Sadness with joy inside—isn't that also remembrance with forgetting inside, the precious forgetting that turns our thoughts in another direction for a moment, that soothes us, opens our eyes to the beauty of the landscape, and allows us to continue on our way in spite of the ghosts around us?

We won't talk about my mother today. It's what she would have wanted. But I know that we'll think about her, each with our own memory of the woman she was. If we had to take turns describing her, we would all paint a different picture. My brothers and I were born from the same body, but we don't have the same mother. A single woman in three people, that is the mystery of motherhood.

Soon we will all be seated around the table, with our laughter, our talk, our stories, just like other years. Every now and then, there will be an old image of her, lost between two sentences, and our eyes will cloud over for a moment before lighting up again. Fortunately, my grandson will be with us, he'll shout out when he gets his presents. He'll remind us of the joyful childhood we had with our mother. She'll be there, among us, like a benevolent spirit, delighted to see us gathered together. I will look at us sitting there eating and drinking, I will say to myself that this woman gave us life with enough light inside to struggle against the darkness.

It's a fine legacy.

References

Page : 7, 175	Gagnon, Madeleine. *Le deuil du soleil*. VLB éditeur, 2011.
Page : 13	Bélanger, Paul. *Replis, chambre de l'arpenteur*. Le Noroît, 2012.
Page : 17, 39, 44	Cohen, Albert. *Le livre de ma mère*. Gallimard, 1974.
Page : 19	Winnicott, Donald Woods. *La mère suffisamment bonne*. Payot, 2006.
Page : 133	Pontalis, Jean-Bertrand. *Un jour, le crime*. Gallimard, 2002.
Page : 134	Émond, Bernard. *Tout ce que tu possèdes*. Lux Éditeur, 2012.
Page : 139, 140	Beauvoir, Simone de. *Une mort très douce*. Gallimard, 1999.
Page : 141	Chamberland, Paul. In *La nuit de la poésie 1970*, by Jean-Claude Labrecque and Jean-Pierre Masse.
Page : 147	Éliacheff, Caroline and Nathalie Heinich. *Mères-filles: une relation à trois*. Livre de Poche, 2003.
Page : 149	Duras, Marguerite. *La vie matérielle*. P.O.L., 1987.
Page : 150	Didi-Huberman, Georges. *Blancs soucis*. Les Éditions de Minuit, 2013.
Page : 156	Barthes, Roland. *Journal de deuil*. Seuil, 2009.
Page : 170	Saint-Denys Garneau, Hector de. *Regards et jeux dans l'espace*. Lux Éditeur, 2005.
Page : 175	Guèvremont, Germaine. *Le Survenant*. BQ, 1990.

Other Works by Louise Dupré translated into English

Fiction

Memoria, novel, translated by Liedewy Hawke. Toronto: Simon & Pierre, 1999.
The Milky Way, novel, translated by Liedewy Hawke. Toronto: Simon & Pierre, 2002.
High-Wire Summer, stories, translated by Liedewy Hawke. Toronto: Cormorant Books, 2009.

Poetry

The Blueness of Light, poems, translated by Antonio D'Alfonso. Toronto: Guernica, 2005.
Beyond the Flames, poems, translated by Antonio D'Alfonso. Toronto: Guernica, 2014.
Rooms, poems, translated by Karen Isabel Ocana. Toronto: Guernica, 2016.
The Haunted Hand, poems, translated by Donald Winkler. Toronto: Guernica, 2020.

Theatre

Just Like Her, text for theatre translated by Erín Moure. Hamilton, ON: Wolsak & Wynn, 2011.

Essays

Theory, a Sunday (with Louky Bersianik, Nicole Brossard, Louise Cotnoir, Gail Scott and France Théoret), essays. New York: Belladonna Series, Inc., 2013.